PRAISE FOR
HEAD IN THE CLOUDS
FEET ON THE GROUND

Ryan has lived this book out and is the perfect person to be delivering this message. This book will provide the tools you need to make your dream a reality.

Levi Lusko, lead pastor of Fresh Life Church
and bestselling author

As a creative person and a dreamer myself, I connected deeply with *Head in the Clouds, Feet on the Ground*. Ryan's insight is right on and will be so helpful to anyone persevering in pursuing a dream. I wish I had this book twenty years ago!

Kristian Stanfill, Passion City Church

Head in the Clouds, Feet on the Ground was such a timely read for me. Ryan authentically encourages the reader never to stop dreaming, offering practical tools for how to move toward that dream all while reminding us that the journey and process are essential to our growth. If you've ever found yourself wondering what's next or have lost the wonder of joining the Dream Giver in fulfilling the adventure he is inviting you into, this book is for you.

Meredith Andrews, worship artist

I love this book! It will inspire you and ground you. You will feel commissioned while being invited to a new level of commitment. Ryan Romeo can be trusted because he has lived big dreams *and* has served faithfully over the long haul.

Jon Egan, worship pastor and songwriter,
New Life Church, Colorado Springs, Colorado

God wants to give you a dream, a dream that changes the world for the better and brings God glory. But so few actually dare to step out into their dreams, to endure the struggle to make them a reality. Ryan wrote this book to help you cultivate your God-given dream. We need you to do it.

I am constantly amazed by how God is using Ryan Romeo. He has not only impacted nearly a million Americans through powerful nights of worship called OUTCRY but is a humble servant of the Lord and the local church. He is used to doing big things for God, but his heart is humbly rooted in the power and miracle of the local church. He is a unique friend with a one-of-a-kind message for you. Don't miss it.

Matt Brown, evangelist, author of *Truth Plus Love*,
founder of Think Eternity

HEAD IN
THE CLOUDS
FEET ON THE GROUND

HEAD IN
THE CLOUDS
FEET ON THE GROUND

A SURVIVAL GUIDE FOR CREATIVES, VISIONARIES, AND DREAMERS

RYAN ROMEO

ZONDERVAN

Head in the Clouds, Feet on the Ground
Copyright © 2020 by Ryan Romeo

Requests for information should be addressed to:
Zondervan, *3900 Sparks Dr. SE, Grand Rapids, Michigan 49546*

Zondervan titles may be purchased in bulk for educational, business, fundraising, or promotional use. For information, please email SpecialMarkets@Zondervan.com.

ISBN 978-0-310-35818-3 (audio)

Library of Congress Cataloging-in-Publication Data

Names: Romeo, Ryan, author.
Title: Head in the clouds, feet on the ground : a survival guide for creatives, visionaries, and
    dreamers / Ryan Romeo.
Description: Grand Rapids : Zondervan, 2020. | Includes bibliographical references. |
    Summary: "Co-founder of the Outcry Worship Tour, Ryan Romeo, knows firsthand the
    challenge of staying hopeful on the journey between a dream and its fulfillment. In
    Head in the Clouds, Feet on the Ground, he'll guide you in finding the right foundation,
    overcoming your dream-killers, and embarking on the most important work of your
    life"-- Provided by publisher.
Identifiers: LCCN 2019034398 (print) | LCCN 2019034399 (ebook) | ISBN 9780310358169
    (trade paperback) | ISBN 9780310358176 (ebook)
Subjects: LCSH: Self-actualization (Psychology)--Religious aspects--Christianity. | Self-
    realization--Religious aspects--Christianity. | Dreams--Religious aspects--Christianity.
Classification: LCC BV4598.2 .R66 2020 (print) | LCC BV4598.2 (ebook) | DDC 248.4--dc23
LC record available at https://lccn.loc.gov/2019034398
LC ebook record available at https://lccn.loc.gov/2019034399

Cover illustration and design: Ash Ulmer Design
Interior illustrations: Ash Ulmer Design
Interior design: Kait Lamphere

Printed in the United States of America

19 20 21 22 23 24 25 26 /LSC/ 15 14 13 12 11 10 9 8 7 6 5 4 3 2 1

✧ ✧

This book is dedicated to my selfless and endlessly patient wife, Blake. She has endured the crazy life of being married to a man with his head in the clouds. It's dedicated to our amazing children, Toby, Adyn, and Mae, who—in the midst of sacrificing much—have adopted their dad's dreams as their own. And I wait expectantly for God to reveal and release them to dreams of their own.

It's dedicated to the most committed and tenacious dreamer I know, my dad, who said to me often, "Ryan, if it were easy, everyone would do it." And to my mom, who always saw more potential in me than I ever saw in myself.

This book is dedicated to the dreamers out there. The elite few who say *yes* to the wild call of the Dream Giver and see the world around them forever changed.

In the end, this book is dedicated to Jesus first and foremost. He has led me on a wild ride. He has brought me to many unexpected and undeserved places. He is the beginning, middle, and end of the life of this dreamer. This book is an overflow of what he has done in my life, and I pray he is pleased above all else with this offering.

CONTENTS

FOREWORD

Growing up, I was always the reluctant dreamer. I didn't want to be let down, and I was afraid to step into anything outside or beyond what might be God's plan for my life.

As a young teenager, I began leading worship in my local church and started writing songs. Leaders started approaching me about leading worship for youth camps and events. At the time, I always needed a ride because I wasn't even old enough to drive yet!

Through all of it, I always simply tried to appreciate the honor of leading worship in my church. I fought to have a right heart and right priorities. My parents always taught me to value the local church and the privilege of leading worship there.

But deep down I was afraid. As I began to have more opportunities, I made sure to protect my heart from letdown. I had dreams but found it hard to believe that God would bring my dreams to pass. I dreamed about diving into the things my heroes were doing. I listened to Delirious? and Sonicflood—music groups that were writing worship songs unlike anything I'd ever heard—and secretly imagined that would be part of *my* calling.

But I continued to doubt and wrestle with fear.

When I was nineteen, I had an independent record out, and I was talking with record labels. It was a dream come true, but instead of being excited, I was afraid of committing and moving forward. I thought, "There is no way God can have this for *me*. It's just too good to be true."

During that time, I was invited to go on a mission trip to the UK. A friend of mine was starting a church and was putting on a big festival. He reached out to me and invited me to come lead worship.

At the end of the festival, rain started to pour down in buckets. Two thousand people proceeded to cram themselves into the only tent in the area. Leaders and sound techs worked frantically to set up a small sound system with one mic and one guitar. The leader turned to me and asked, "Can you lead a few songs?" Reluctantly, I stepped forward. The moment I began to sing—*boom*—the power went out. Two thousand people were crammed into a tent in the pitch-black.

Amid the chaos, something came over me, and at the top of my lungs, I sang an old familiar song, "I love you, Lord. And I lift my voice . . ." As I sang, a hurricane of voices hit me in response. The tent filled with powerful praises to God. I held back tears as we sang. And just as we wrapped up the song—". . . let it be a sweet, sweet sound in your ears"—the power came back on. It was like a perfectly timed scene from a movie. It was like the day of Pentecost. It was a God-timed moment of power. I then led an hour of worship, just me and a guitar, and it became one of the best moments of my life.

That evening, I heard the still small voice of God. "Don't be afraid to walk into the calling I have for you. I've dreamed up something beautiful for your life, so don't be afraid to step into it. I've created you to dream. I've created you to have the same dreams I have for you."

That day I became aware of God's heart for me, God's heart for us all. I realized *he* has a vision. *He* has a dream—not only for me but for the church and for the world. And I realized he wants us to link arms with him to see *his* dream come to pass, and that huge global dream included his dream for me.

After that, I simply said *yes* to God's vision for my life, finally embracing that secret dream I had carried at arms-length for years. I dove into the things that had scared me so much before.

Ryan's book reminded me that we all have to conquer fear to step into the God-given dreams in our lives. It's not just "follow your dreams;" it's following God's dreams for you. It's not do what you want; it's aligning your heart with what he wants for you.

Ryan has lived this out and walked into some huge dreams. He knows the fear, and he knows what it feels like when you finally believe and trust enough to step into God's dreams for you. This book is full of both God-centered inspiration and practical insights that will leave you built up and help you move forward in your God-given dreams and callings.

I pray that this book empowers you to take the same step that I did all those years ago. I pray that it empowers you to say yes to God's dreams for your life.

Phil Wickham, worship artist

AN INVITATION TO DREAM

I have a guilty pleasure—one I tend to keep hidden from most people.

I daydream about it.

I make detailed and outlandish plans about it.

I google and Pinterest-board it.

This hidden part of me is absolutely obsessed. Obsessed with this one powerful thing—*zombies*.

All things zombie, in fact. I often stay up late to watch a zombie movie by myself—because it's probably no surprise that my wife certainly won't watch it with me. I scan Amazon on my Kindle to find the latest zombie novels. I even follow zombie accounts on Instagram. Movies, books, social media, *whatever*. I love to dive into anything that explores the dark underbelly of human survival when the world is overrun by hordes of the flesh-eating undead.

Most zombie tales tell some version of the same story—everyday city dwellers trying to survive in a postapocalyptic world. There's no more electricity. No more grocery stores. No more internet. There are only formerly urban people doing their best not to become zombie snacks.

I can't help but wonder how I would survive in such a hostile, dog-eat-dog world. I'd have to learn new skills, go back to basics, gain a new understanding of the world around me. Otherwise, I might find myself the victim of a flesh-eating ghoul. I'd have to face nearly insurmountable odds just to live another day.

To be honest, this kind of scenario isn't all that different from what I have to do every day to survive as a dreamer. Well, except for the ghoul part.

It may sound melodramatic, but when I'm chasing a big or crazy dream, I always end up facing some of my greatest struggles. And as it is in a zombie apocalypse, I have to learn new skills. I have to gain a new understanding of the world around me. I have to be prepared to overcome whatever it is out there that wants to kill my dream and kick me to the sidelines.

If you're a dreamer, I'm guessing you can relate.

You know what it's like to dream big dreams, to imagine new possibilities, to constantly wonder, What if?—and then to hit the struggles and the smackdowns. Maybe you've chased some dreams and found that nothing was as easy or as glamorous as you imagined. Perhaps you made some mistakes and feel as though you're somehow disqualified from dreaming big again. Or maybe you're so overwhelmed by the bigness of the dream that you find it impossible to take even a first step. Whatever the dream may be, every dreamer has to struggle and fight to survive—and a lot of us don't make it. That's why one of the greatest challenges you will ever face is the journey between a dream and its fulfillment.

Another thing I've learned from zombie stories—I promise I'll stop talking about zombies after this—is that those who do manage to survive the initial zombie onslaught inevitably have to face what might be an even greater threat: other survivors.

The people who are left eventually find themselves fighting one another for food, water, and shelter. The fight for resources and basic survival will begin to forge alliances and create enemies. At some point the zombies become a mere distraction compared with the struggle to simply *survive* with other people.

It's the same for dreamers. Even when we develop all the dreamer combat skills we need to survive—hard work, vision-casting, and leadership—we still have to face the dangers that come from other people. More often than not, it's people who feel threatened by our dreams because they have abandoned their own. When we're getting our dreams off the ground, it amplifies the disappointment or even bitterness they feel for not having done so in their own lives. Such people, often those closest to us, then become our harshest critics.

Often the church is the best place to learn this firsthand.

A FIGHT FOR SURVIVAL

I was attending a church of about two hundred people when I had my first big dream—a vision for my future that I knew didn't originate with me. It was a calling, one much greater than anything I could accomplish on my own. I was involved with the worship team and was a leader in the youth group. I was still a young Christian and spent a lot of time poring over the Bible and learning from my leaders. I was also struggling to do ministry with people who didn't think as I did because they were from a different generation or a different cultural background. I was learning the beautiful, difficult struggle of life in the local church. But deep down, I knew I was destined for more.

It wasn't that I believed I was entitled to more or that what I was doing wasn't important. I knew it might take decades for my dream to come to pass. I also knew that what I did in that small church affected the outcome of my bigger dream—that what I did in the small and the everyday really did impact the big and the someday. But I also knew deep down in my bones that there was more to come.

So I walked around with my head in the clouds. I listened to Delirious or Passion or David Crowder—pure late-nineties worship goodness—and felt that that was a world I'd one day be in. I imagined big crowds of people and worship events that would change everyone who attended—events that would show the world the love we had for Jesus and the love we had for one another.

That was my dream. I had a deep passion for events that centered on worship and a passion for the church. In all its beautiful vagueness, that is what I felt called to. I didn't know how I'd get there. Didn't know what I'd be doing once I got there. Didn't know how to make it happen. I knew only that I felt called to it.

The problem? I lived in Tucson, Arizona, for one. Not exactly a place flourishing with big opportunities for worship events. Not even a place with many Christians, let alone a place to gather many Christians. *Wasn't this sort of dream supposed to come from Nashville or LA?*

I was also in a small church. A little church with, honestly, no aspirations of becoming a big church. *Wasn't this sort of dream supposed to come from a megachurch or a music promoter?*

And I didn't have any connections—or even any hope of making those connections. I didn't know anybody of influence in the Christian music world. *Wasn't this sort of dream supposed to come from a well-connected insider?*

There was literally nothing around me to indicate I was on the right path. I was a tumbleweed drifting in the desert of nowhere (not to be melodramatic).

Nevertheless, I took a risk and shared my dream with the people around me—to mixed reviews. A couple of people were encouraging, but many told me it was a pipe dream. "Everyone wants to do things like that," they said, looking at me as if I were a child who'd said he wanted to live in a candy factory. They smiled and tried to be kind, but the thought bubbles over their heads said something more like, "This deluded young man has a big dream but has no idea how difficult the real world is."

The other survivors.

What hurt the worst was that what they said was basically true—I had no reason to believe I could achieve such an impossible dream. Their words eroded my feeling of being called. The faith-filled corner of my heart that believed God would equip me for such a calling crumbled. I didn't know it at the time, but I'd just run headlong into dream killers, otherwise known as seemingly insurmountable circumstances—or in my case, critics. External critics pointed out my greatest insecurities, and internal critics—the voices in my head that told me that those critics were right—threatened to relegate me to the sidelines. These and other hostile forces came together for one purpose—to kill the dream God had placed in me.

Fortunately, the dream killers failed. Eventually, I discovered that obstacles that seem huge and insurmountable when they are right in front of me appear much smaller in the rearview mirror.

After nearly twenty years, my initial dream has come to pass, beyond anything I could have imagined. Nearly one million people attended the OUTCRY worship tour. Tens of thousands have been saved. Tens of thousands of kids were freed from the cycle of poverty. And as amazing as those numbers have been to experience, seeing the dream I had long ago come to pass is truly the greatest privilege. And I truly believe my best chapters are yet to be lived.

KEEP YOUR HEAD IN THE CLOUDS *AND* YOUR FEET ON THE GROUND

Over the years, I've learned a few survival tactics. I've learned how to silence the dream killers. I've learned that their attacks are predictable and uncreative. I've learned that God wants to build a foundation in us before we can embark on the calling he has for us. The work required to build this foundation isn't boring homework or head-patting busywork. It's real work, and it matters because the quality of the foundation we build is the difference between life and death for our dream.

You need to know two things about building this kind of foundation. First, God gave you your dreams. God already knows everything about you. He does not care where you come from. He knows your past. He isn't clueless. He knows the seemingly hopeless situation you may be in right now. Whatever it is you're up against, he *knows*. And he still gives you dreams. In fact, he is more committed to seeing your dreams come to pass than you are. You are in safe hands! Never let your "seemingly insurmountable circumstances" derail the "what-if" dreams in your heart. *Keep your head in the clouds.*

The second thing you need to know is this: your habits in the short term impact your calling in the long term. Today matters, even when it doesn't feel like it—*especially* when it doesn't feel like it. How you treat your current job—and how you treat your current boss—matters. How hard you work right now matters.

If you think it's okay to give 50 percent of your effort to what you're doing now because you're waiting until your "ultimate calling" to give 100 percent, you're laying a cracked foundation from the start. The truth is that you'll end up giving half your effort for the rest of your life because that's all your foundation can support.

Remember the parable of the talents? If not, check it out in Matthew 25:14–30. The bottom line is that Jesus expects us to invest whatever talents or resources he gives us. Invest *now*, not later. Do the hard work, put in the time, develop the skills— whatever it takes to get a return on what's been entrusted to you. The journey to your dreams may be long and filled with circumstances that don't make sense, but keep going. You must work hard with what you have now. *Keep your feet on the ground.*

This book is meant to empower and equip you to do both—to keep your head in the clouds and keep your feet on the ground. I want to help you keep your dreams alive, even when the dream killers try to relegate you and your dreams to the sidelines. And I want to help you do the hard work of building a foundation for your dream. No one else can keep your dream alive if you let it die, and the foundation for your dream will not build itself.

Any dream built on a faulty foundation is almost certain to come crashing down. And even if it doesn't crash, it will be stunted because a dream can grow only to the size that your foundation can handle. That's why achieving your dream begins with giving 100 percent to the seemingly small and unimportant things. That's how you keep your feet on the ground and your head in the clouds right from the start. And this is a habit you can begin now.

This book is organized into three parts, each of which empowers and equips you to take the next step toward your dreams. In Part 1: The Groundwork, we dive into the foundation: the heart-level perspectives and habit-changing skills you will need on your journey. Part 2: The Dream Killers tackles the difficulties you can anticipate so that when they hit, you'll be prepared to hit back. Part 3: Start is about how to dive into your dreams with what you have in your hands right now, trusting that God will use whatever that is to move you from dreaming into walking in your calling.

I can't wait to dive in. This will be more fun than building a postapocalyptic survival bunker. So let's go!

PART 1

THE GROUNDWORK

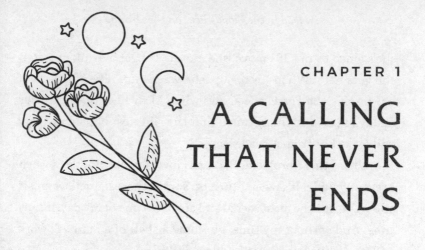

CHAPTER 1

A CALLING THAT NEVER ENDS

It's early morning, and I'm lying awake in bed, staring at the ceiling. I feel trapped. I want to go to the kitchen to get a cup of coffee and read, to have a moment of solitude before the chaos of my day begins, but I can't move. A small but mighty force has me pinned down.

My six-year-old daughter, Mae.

Most nights, Mae-Mae's* small silhouette appears in our bedroom doorway around three in the morning. In the dim backlight, she appears to be more hair than child. After pausing for a moment, she stumbles across the room and into our bed. Once she lies down on the pillow we have ready for her—like I said, she does this a lot—she quietly reaches out for my hand so she can fall back asleep.

It warms my heart, and I treasure these moments because I know there will come a day when she won't do this anymore. But as heart-warming as it is, from the moment she takes my hand,

---

*Not a typo. Her name is so short we have to use it twice.

she's glued to me. If I move, she moves. If I get a drink of water, she gets hers. When I wake up, she wakes up. Like a little Jedi harnessing the Force, she knows when I leave her presence. Her daddy radar is so finely tuned that the slightest blip on my part will wake her from a dead sleep.

Why is this a problem? Because I love my mornings. It's when I read my Bible. It's when I turn on some ethereal, mellow music and write. It's the most sacred and creative time of my day. It's my time. And without my time, I become a shell of a man. All work and no quiet time makes Daddy a dull boy.

Now, there are ways to divert her, but they aren't always easy to pull off. For example, to keep her sleeping and happy, I've made a bed for her on the living room couch or on the eat-in bench in our kitchen so she can have the satisfaction of still being close to me while I read and write. Trust me, I do anything I can to divert that sweet little time thief just so I can have a moment to myself.

Having time to myself in the morning is crucial because my wife and I live in a swirl of (mostly happy) chaos. Blake and I have three small kids, and we both work full time at a church. On top of that, I write, produce a podcast, and tour. I feel exhausted just writing that down. Our day-to-day life is nuts. From the time the children are up until the time they go to bed, there are very few moments to be still, to have an uninterrupted thought, or to just breathe.

But when I'm in the center of that hurricane, no matter how crazy a situation gets, I can't avoid this one thing:

I am a dreamer.

Most mornings (once I find a nearby base for Mae-Mae), my dreams meet me. The beautiful what-ifs start to flood in, and I feel the excitement of both the dreams that are already off the ground and the ones that are yet to be. Dreams are what stir my heart and make me come alive. I love almost nothing more than the challenge of creating something new out of nothing, of seeing a vision move from my imagination to reality. And I know I'm not the only one.

I believe that deep down in their heart, every person has a childlike dream. You feel its presence deep in your bones. No matter how crazy your life gets, it whispers to you whenever you are still and quiet. It is a dream that seems beyond your reach, one that seems foolish even to say out loud. But you can't keep it quiet. It sneaks into your thoughts in the middle of the night or on your morning commute. It slips out in conversations with friends and family. It stirs within you a profound longing to live with the freedom and confidence of knowing you were made for this.

And yet . . .

We live in the tension between where we are and where we want to go. The tension between the beauty of our dreams and the starkness of our reality. The tension between the person we are now and the person we want to become.

Some of this is just life. We will always have new ground to take and new places to go. And that's a good thing. It keeps us yearning, hoping, and growing. But our dreams also give us a glimpse into the Father's heart for us. He wants more for us. All by itself, that longing you feel for something more is often the first hint that you are being called to pursue a dream. I firmly believe I have a calling and so do you. When you accept God's invitation to pursue your dreams, the journey it takes you on is your life—the life you were made for.

Here's a promise, one I can make from experience. Pursuing your God-given dreams is one of the greatest challenges you will ever have in life—but it's worth it. Think of it as a wide-open job position written just for you. Nobody else is even going to apply for it. It's a life that was handcrafted by God, and it has your name on it.

At this point I'm guessing you might be thinking something like this: Is this another self-help book? One promising that all my wildest dreams will come true if I just think enough happy thoughts or hustle enough?

The short answer is no. That's not what I'm saying. Following your dream isn't a mix of happy thoughts and hustle; it's taking the first of many steps on a journey. It's the catalytic thought or desire that propels you into a calling that never ends, a calling with a thousand twists and turns that keeps you on the edge of your seat and never reaches an ultimate destination. Because God's calling is not a destination; it's a journey.

That's the short answer.

The long answer is what you'll read throughout the rest of this book.

I was recently talking with a friend about God's will and what it means to have a calling from God. "Our idea of an ultimate 'calling' is really just a modern construct," he said. "When you look at the Bible, you don't see our modern perspective of having just one ultimate life calling."

"I agree." I said. "But it's hard to let go of. Most of us have had the idea of one calling or one job drilled into us since childhood. It starts when the grown-ups duck down to our level and ask, 'So, what do you want to be when you grow up?'"

My friend replied, "And it doesn't help that a lot of us have been told, 'You can do anything you want if you put your mind to it. We grew up and discovered that this isn't always true. Just because you have a degree doesn't mean you can get a job. And just because you have a job doesn't mean you won't be laid off. The idea that a college degree or a few years of hustle is a straight path to success is a fantasy—and it's left a whole generation of us feeling burned and cynical about pursuing our dreams."

I get it. And you've probably seen it too. But we need to make sure we don't throw the baby out with the bathwater. In other words, we don't want to throw out a God-given dream because of some soggy disappointments and cynicism.

So let me circle back to what my friend said about the idea of a calling being a modern construct rather than a biblical one. When I look at the Bible and read the history of God and his people, I see a pattern that looks something like this:

- God gives someone a grand dream or vision of something they—and their friends and family—never imagined they could do.
- This person's life gets hard and takes a lot of unexpected twists and turns and seems to go in the opposite direction of said grand dream.
- Then, after a period of toil and hardship, the dream is realized, just as God originally said it would be.

And you don't have to take my word for it. Read the stories, and check it out for yourself. This is the pattern of how things went with Joseph, Sarah, David, and Gideon. And it will probably be the same pattern with you. People who receive dreams and visions from

God inevitably have to wait, persevere, struggle, and work hard before their dreams are realized. It's a pattern that's persisted now for thousands of years, and I don't see it changing anytime soon.

Here's the misguided idea we need to reconsider about dreams. Many of us talk about God's calling or the dream he has for us as if it's some distant, yet-to-be-attained thing. It is perpetually in the future, not the present. It is ever before us, just beyond reach. It will be realized only on some magical day in the future when all the stars align, our circumstances are rosy, and everything feels perfect.

Until that day, the longing for our dream stalks us, nags at us, all the while reminding us that we aren't quite there yet. We might try to make sense of this by imagining that God is testing us. We reason that when we pass the test, then—and only then—will God open this elusive door to our dreams and let us in. Or we might reason instead that God is actively blocking our progress because it somehow isn't godly to dream big dreams. We imagine that God will be satisfied only when we set our dreams aside and walk in "humility" by keeping our head down and our passions hidden.

I sometimes refer to these ways of thinking as the dreamer's roller coaster. We soar up on the momentum of faith, passion, and adrenaline. Then we plummet down the slope of doubt, fear, disappointment, and shame. We might make some minor adjustments, but then we repeat the same thing all over again. Up and down on a mental, emotional, and spiritual rollercoaster that leaves us some combination of nauseous and nowhere.

It's time to exit that crazy ride. It's time to trade in the misguided ideas for something better—for Someone better. So here's my pep talk for you.

I believe in you. I believe in your dream. I believe in your calling. I believe you are fully equipped to start walking toward your dream today. Because your calling is happening right now. Your dreams, talents, and skills are to be walked in and walked toward today. Your dream isn't only for future you, it's for current you. The now you.

Let me take another guess at what you might be thinking. How can you say that, Ryan? We don't even know each other. How can you say you believe in me?

You're right! I don't know you. I don't know all your baggage and history. I don't know where you live or where you came from. I don't know how many Instagram followers you have or what you did last summer.

But here's what I do know, which is the foundation for this book: I believe in the *Dream Giver*. God is the momentum shifter and vision caster for your life. I don't need to know you to know that God is the source of every worthwhile dream you have. That's how I can say with full confidence that I believe in you, I believe in your dream, and I believe in your calling. Because your calling is at the intersection of your dream and God's power. And as you walk in that calling, you realize that God saw those things first. He is the one who dreamed your dream for you. He is the one who planted that dream-seed deep in your heart in the first place. He is the owner and originator of every worthwhile dream. That means your role as a dreamer is not so much about taking ownership of your dream as it is taking stewardship of your dream. Your job is to take responsibility for the dream that ultimately belongs to God but is entrusted to you.

This is so important: before you take the first step to get your dream off the ground, you must understand *who you are* relative to *who God is*. You must see yourself through his lens. You must see your dreams, gifts, and calling through his eyes. You must exit the dreamer's roller coaster and anchor yourself to the Dream Giver's firm foundation.

Build your hope on the Dream Giver so you can pursue your dream with confidence. We will come back to this idea again and again because it's something every dreamer needs to be reminded of—daily. Especially when we face dream killers such as the Critic, the Noise, and the Setback, all of which we'll talk about in part 2. To survive in a dog-eat-dog world and among enemies trying to take down our dreams, we must continually set our sights on God. Doing so is a habit of the heart that helps us put our confidence where it belongs—in the unchanging character of the Dream Giver.

God is the one who created you. He fashioned you in your mother's womb. He chased after you when you were lost. He knows everything about you—the person he made you to be. He never does anything without purpose, including creating you. He knows the *true* you. The you that is buried under guilt and mistakes. The you that is buried under the person you think you should be. The you that is buried under the careless words of friends or family that hurt you when you were young. The guilt, mistakes, and careless words aren't you. They're piles of dirt that have been shoveled over you, shoveled over the person God sees when he looks at you.

You are God's work of art. It says so in the Bible: "We are his workmanship, created in Christ Jesus for good works, which God prepared beforehand, that we should walk in them" (Ephesians 2:10 ESV).

God has recreated you through Jesus to be the true you—who you were always destined to be. He made good plans and dreamed good dreams for you before you were born. He longs to see you—his child—walk in those plans and realize those dreams. Jesus didn't save you just so you would go to heaven; he saved you to reveal the *you* who you were always meant to be. He wants to unearth the real you, the one liberated from the shackles of the world and the fear of others' opinions.

The you that is truly free.

The moment you believe this—a deep-down, feel-it-in-your-bones sort of believing—your life will begin to change.

And the key to believing is to consistently keep your mindset on the character of the Dream Giver. He is your source of all confidence and your greatest friend. So bring him into this process. Invite his insight. Ask for his help. He won't fail you.

THE
DREAMER

Before we dive in, let's take a step back and talk about the dreamer's mindset—the way you think about your dream.

Remember, to pursue your dreams, you have to keep your head in the clouds and your feet on the ground. That's a mindset as well as a framework for pursuing your dreams. And it's not easy to do. Especially when disappointments and detours try to yank your head out of the clouds. Or when the unfun demands of reality try to knock your feet off the ground.

The temptation is to choose one or the other—clouds or ground. At their most extreme, these are opposites on a dreamer continuum. Go too far toward one, and you'll risk losing your dream to bitter pessimism; go too far toward the other, and you'll risk drowning it in foggy optimism. The goal is to stay balanced by avoiding either extreme. Even though they are opposites, the end result of falling into either extreme mindset is the same: *You stop pursuing your dream.*

TWO EXTREME DREAM MINDSETS

Let's tackle these two extreme dream mindsets that we need to avoid. I've typecast them into two fictional characters because it's a lot more fun that way. Allow me to introduce Anti-Head-in-the-Clouds Curmudgeon and Everything-Should-Be-Easy Optimist.

Anti-Head-in-the-Clouds Curmudgeon

Curmudgeon takes his life very seriously. His motto is the old adage "Life is hard and then you die—and go to heaven, of course." There are no beautiful what-ifs in his heart because he has life figured out. Ask him about his dreams, and he'll use his grumpy old man voice to shut you down. "God is more interested in building my character than filling my head with nonsense. He wants me to act with good behavior, not to go off chasing some fluffy dreams."

Curmudgeon easily goes into lecture mode and will do his best to lower your expectations of life as well. "You little whippersnappers have no idea how hard the real world is. I had to walk uphill both ways in the snow without shoes to give up on my dreams. Take it from me, you need to give up on those dreams of yours now so you can be a mature, miserable grownup like me!"

A bit over the top? Okay, maybe. But Curmudgeon's attitude is one that can be found in men and women of any age and in all areas of life. Curmudgeon can be sneaky too. Many times his philosophies are under the surface. Often they are more felt than communicated. But his effect on a workplace, family, or church is undeniable. When Curmudgeon is in charge, the community becomes a graveyard of dreams, a hardened support group for the ex-dreamers.

Whenever we hear Curmudgeon's voice grumping around in our thoughts and trying to get our head out of the clouds, we need to remember a few things about the character of the Dream Giver.

Now, of course God is interested in building our character,

but only because he's trying to prepare us for the dreams he himself placed in our hearts. Curmudgeon has it backward. God wants to build our character because he wants us to have everything we need to walk into our dreams and callings. Remember, it is God who gives the dream and creates the dreamer. We love him because he first loved us. God is a good Father who is more committed to our dreams than we are.

Here's a promise you can rely on when the curmudgeons get you down. The Bible tells us that the God who began a good work within you will continue it and bring it to completion (Philippians 1:6). The dream he started in your heart will bear fruit in time. It will take years of work. It will have dark and difficult seasons. But God's promise remains: if he started it, he'll finish it.

But if we approach our dreams with the mindset that *God* is a grumpy curmudgeon whose only interest is to build our character, then we will never fully realize the God-given potential of our lives. God isn't only in the character-building business. He's in the people-building business. He's in the dream-giving business. *And* he's in the dream-fulfilling business.

Everything-Should-Be-Easy Optimist

Okay. Now let's consider extreme dream mindset number two: Everything-Should-Be-Easy Optimist.

Optimist is, well, optimistic. A little too optimistic. Her motto is "A fulfilled dream is a dreamer's right." Ask her about her dreams, and she'll get a faraway look in her eyes. "My dream doesn't require any work," she'll chuckle with incredulity. "It's all up to the Lord. I'm just sitting back waiting for my perfect ship to roll in."

Ask her for advice, and Optimist is quick with platitudes

and spiritual warm fuzzies. "Don't worry so much about working toward your dreams," she'll say. "If God is in it, then little to no work is required (by me anyway). Besides, any work other than prayer is striving in the flesh, which is sinful." She'll go on to tell you there's no need for all that networking, planning, and pitching of your ideas. "Let's just pray about it," she'll say with a wave of her hand. "When you stop trying so hard, you can be sure it is of God and not your flesh when your dreams are finally fulfilled." And *if* visions do begin to be fulfilled in Optimist's life—though it's built on the hard work of other people—she'll smile and say, "See, why were you all working so hard?"

I know, I know, it's extreme. But I've talked to many people whose mindset isn't too far off from this. Let's call this extreme mindset what it is, which is entitled laziness wrapped in Christian language.

Optimist's attitude may seem spiritual, but it actually causes you to stop pursuing your dream because you (if you are the optimist) feel entitled to other people's work and buy-in. Left unchecked, it will create the unrealistic expectation that everyone else should share your dream. You may begin to feel that if you are passionate about something, your leaders or friends should be passionate about it too. *What's wrong with them that they don't seem to "get it"?* This is when entitlement creeps in. *If everyone around me "got it," then they would work for my dream—because I certainly am not.* This is when the self-centered self-righteousness creeps in.

Optimist lives with her head in the clouds. She also lives with her feet in the clouds too. And the sad irony is that this perspective can cause you to give up on your dream.

Whenever we hear the fuzzy whispers of Optimist wafting through our thoughts and trying to knock our feet off the ground, we need to recenter our mindset on the character of the Dream Giver.

Our dreams are *our* dreams and *our* responsibility. Other people may or may not understand or share our dreams—and that's okay! There are as many dreams as there are people out there, and your leaders and friends have their own dreams that they are passionate about and responsible for. We are not entitled to other people's passion and commitment. If we want shared passion and commitment, we earn that by showing people our dream and casting a vision for it (which we'll talk more about later).

All this requires work. Hard work. Feet-on-the-ground work. If we approach our dreams by putting everything on "God's shoulders," we miss out on the amazing privilege it is to be co-laborers with God. We miss our opportunity to see the fruit of the gifts and talents God invested in us. Healthy work doesn't negate the Holy Spirit; it *confirms* his hand in our creation. It confirms that he wired you and me to walk in the dreams he had for us before the foundations of the world. It shows that we are *equipped*. Spirit-filled work can be just as miraculous as spirit-filled interjection from God. And this is the power of work that Optimist misses out on.

A PROPHETIC ECHO

Curmudgeon and Optimist are opposite extremes, but hanging out with either one of them will lead you to the exact same place.

Giving up.

Since you picked up a book about pursuing your dreams, I'm hoping that means you haven't given up yet. Mazel tov.

So, where are you when it comes to your dreams?

Even if you haven't given up on dreaming, it could be that you haven't had a clear and specific dream since you were a kid. Maybe you've been quietly holding on to a dream for decades, and now it seems further away than ever. Or maybe you are just setting out on your journey and have no idea where to begin. Wherever you are, I want to stress again how much God cares about your dream. He gave you your dream on purpose and for a purpose.

And one more thing you must understand: the dream in your heart is only a *prophetic echo* of your calling. By prophetic echo, I mean that pursuing your dream may reveal an even deeper dream that God has for you. As you begin to pursue God-given dreams with everything you've got, there's a good chance God will begin to direct your path in new ways.

This is the difference between a calling and dreaming. Dreaming is the echo, or prompting, that propels you to step out. It gives you the general idea or direction. Calling is that God-planned season that you actually live out. Dreaming is the sign to the path. Calling is the *path itself*.

God can't direct your path if you aren't moving. That's why actively pursuing your dreams is so vital. It's the *start* of the journey. It's the spark that gets you moving. It's the catalyst that will thrust you into God's call for your life. And if you understand that God's love and purposefulness is always at work, you can trust him and be flexible when he sends you on an unexpected path. At least, that's how it was for me.

It was a big night. I was backstage pacing back and forth, going over my notes. I was riddled with anxiety. My mouth was dry, my heart was racing, my mind was clicking through questions. *What am I supposed to say? Oh, yeah. Talk about the heart behind this tour, and what else? Oh, yeah. Thank our sponsors. Wait, am I forgetting something? Why am I doing this again?*

I could hear music going on behind me. That was a good thing. It meant I had more time. Behind me twenty thousand people were singing their hearts out to Jesus. I had waited and worked many years for this moment. But, if I were being honest, this moment wasn't exactly what I had in mind. I felt as if I was trying to write with the wrong hand. As if this was almost my dream, but not quite.

I was on the concert tour I'd always dreamed about, but instead of leading worship, which I was comfortable doing, God shifted me to leading behind the scenes and speaking. This was not something I felt *equipped* for. Not something I felt *prepared* for. And certainly not something I felt *comfortable* doing. At all.

Suddenly, the crowd exploded with applause. The music had stopped. That meant I was up. My heart skipped a beat. My palms began to sweat. *Wait, what am I supposed to say again?*

That was the night we launched an event called OUTCRY, a worship tour featuring all my heroes—Hillsong, Bethel, Jesus Culture, Passion, Lauren Daigle, Kari Jobe, and many more. It was a worship tour with a heart for the local church. And that first year of the tour, over 150,000 people came out for it. This was my absolute dream come true.

Well, almost.

I had always dreamed of doing a tour like OUTCRY, but, as I said, what I imagined and what I ended up doing were two different things. Pursuing my dream of a worship tour led me to a different dream, to the calling God had for me, which was speaking and leading the tour rather than leading worship. It stemmed from pursuing my dream, but I had to be willing to shift when God made it clear he had something else for me.

Since then, I've written a book about the tour, cleverly titled *OUTCRY*. I've also met with leaders all over the country and have spoken in front of nearly a million people. God's ultimate dream for me was bigger and far better than mine. But I never would have discovered it if I hadn't pursued my initial dream with everything I had. Leading worship at large events was my prophetic echo. And it was only when I started walking toward it that God could reveal more.

On top of that, I would never have gotten to this point had I not spent years building my spiritual foundation before I ever went out on my first tour. It was in those years of pain and tenacity that I learned to trust God's character and to see myself and my calling through his lens. That's when I came to believe deep in my bones that God cares about my dreams and is more committed to them than I am. And it became a powerful belief that propelled me into a wild and amazing journey. And I believe that if you're willing to believe this yourself, it will lead you on your own wild and amazing journey. Your current situation may not look like you thought it would. You will no doubt take unexpected left and right turns. But God is faithful to reveal more of his bigger dream for you along the way. And it all begins when you say yes to that prophetic echo.

Sadly, I've met many people who believe that God's call is to *deny* their dreams and passions. To take the deep-down dream in their heart and sacrifice it on the altar. And when they use that kind of spiritual language, it *seems* right. It *seems* noble. It *seems* Jesusy. But I think the truth is that this is a perspective rooted more in fear than faith. It may sound right, but it won't produce much fruit in a person's life. It's only another misguided whisper from the Everything-Should-Be-Easy Optimist.

Now, don't get me wrong, following Jesus *does* have a price. A big one. And it will no doubt require great sacrifice and patience from you. God will also reveal selfish and self-exalting aspects of your dream that must be burned away. Sometimes painfully. But the notion that God wants you to sacrifice your entire dream does not line up with what I know about the character of the Dream Giver.

So why does this misguided mindset persist? Why do so many of us seem to think denying the dreams God gives us is somehow pleasing to God?

I think it stems in part from a misunderstanding of what Jesus meant when he said, "Whoever wants to be my disciple must deny themselves and take up their cross and follow me" (Matthew 16:24). We also know that Jesus said, "In this world you will have trouble" (John 16:33). These are not fun to hear. This is not the picture of a happy-go-lucky life with Jesus fulfilling our dreams. So I get it. I understand how some people might come to the conclusion that we need to deny ourselves anything in this life that brings any joy or fulfillment.

But . . .

Dying to yourself does not mean dying to the God-wired, God-purposed portion of your life. I need you to hear this: when you give your life to Jesus, you do not lose the unique and beautiful things God created inside you. You amplify them. The crazy truth is that when you lose your life for Jesus, you gain it back with interest. You gain the true you back. Dying to yourself does not mean dying to the God-given dreams in your life. It does not mean sacrificing the skills and talents and uniqueness of the person he created you to be.

So what *does* it mean to deny ourselves? It means to follow Christ in his mission of sacrificial love. It means to set aside anything that keeps us from saying an empowered yes to the person we were created to be and to become. And what does that look like when we're chasing a big dream? It might mean sacrificing a desire to be famous so we can say yes to God using us behind the scenes. It might mean sacrificing a desire to be comfortable and unchallenged so we can say yes to God's teaching us perseverance and wisdom. It might mean sacrificing finances or free time so we can say yes to the God-dream. Do you see how these require a death to self but also a life-affirming yes to God?

Make no mistake, pursuing your dreams will likely be one of the hardest pursuits of your life. It will be a crucible of character that burns away whatever it is that isn't part of the true you. Those are the things—and there may be many—that God wants you to sacrifice. Each one will require humility. Each one will require a death—a dying to self-will—that will hurt. And each one will ultimately help you say a deeper yes to God and the dreams he has for you.

But none will require the sacrifice of your *calling*. Your calling is not your own. It is a dream that originates in God, not you. Remember, you are the steward, not the owner, of your dream. This is the same principle the apostle Paul used when he wrote, "Do you not know that your bodies are temples of the Holy Spirit, who is in you, whom you have received from God? You are not your own; you were bought at a price. Therefore honor God with your bodies" (1 Corinthians 6:19–20).

Now, I understand the context of this verse is not talking about your dreams. But the principle is the same—*you are not your own.* You were bought at a great price. You belong to someone else. And that Someone Else has invested dreams, talents, and attributes in you that he wants you to run with. He held a dream in his hands, lined up everyone on earth, and then pointed right to you and said, "I entrust this dream to you." He wants you to love this dream and to live it, not sacrifice it.

But what happens when you do deny your dreams? What is the fruit of the life that has repressed its God-given vision?

THE DREAM REPRESSOR

There are many people out there who have repressed their God-given dreams in the name of being "faithful to God." But to believe that God wants you to kill the seed he planted in you makes no sense. God cares more for that seed than you do. And he is committed to seeing to it that what he planted in you yields fruit.

That means that denying or sacrificing your God-given dreams has consequences. If you choose to repress the dreams and visions God gives you, you will damage your heart. Over time, instead of becoming softer to God and more loving to others, you will grow increasingly callous and increasingly threatened by the freedom in other people's lives. You will become some version of the resentful, disappointed curmudgeon. Instead of seeing yourself as a steward responsible for shepherding your dream through challenges, you will see yourself as a victim of every circumstance—the "bad" boss, the difficult childhood, the lack of resources. Eventually, you'll be a shadow of the true person God wants you to be, someone who nurses an angry resentment that you never got your shot at success. Even worse, you will be filled with a compulsion to drag others down too. *Why should they have their dreams if I can't have mine?* At this point, you will have officially become one of the "other survivors." Welcome to the zombie apocalypse.

Those who repress God-given dreams will go one of two ways. Let's go back to our extremes.

First, you may become the Curmudgeon. You will begin to thrive only on the "realistic" and subconsciously set out to destroy those optimistic dreamers around you. You will begin to feel joy from squashing those "kids" with their heads in the clouds.

The other way you could go is the self-protective avoidance that the Optimist operates in. You may be happy on the outside, but on the inside you are riddled with fear and insecurity. You may be speaking with spiritual optimism, but on the inside you don't want to allow yourself to dare start working on your dream. Preparation is an act of faith you are not willing to dive into.

If you find yourself slipping down one of those paths (which we all do from time to time), it's vital to recenter your mindset on the character of the Dream Giver.

If you are slipping down the path of the Curmudgeon, anchor yourself to the mindset that God is for you and not against you. You will begin to champion not only your dreams but the dreams of those around you. Challenge yourself to dream with others, and practice encouraging, not discouraging, those around you.

If you are slipping down the path of the Optimist, start by

choosing to see *every day* as your shot at success. Start moving away from fear and toward a dream you believe God has given you. Your ultimate act of faith will be preparing for the thing you've been praying for.

Dream repression can be a dangerous thing for the dreamer. But we also need to take a look at our actual dream as well. Every worthwhile dream you have originates with God, but not all dreams are worthwhile. If you want to run flat out and with full confidence toward your dream, you need to make sure that your dream doesn't stink.

DREAMS THAT STINK

Hook Hand: Go, live your dream.
Flynn Rider: I will.
Hook Hand: Your dream stinks. I was talking to her.
(Motions to Rapunzel.)

If you've seen the Disney movie *Tangled*, then you know the story behind this dialog. I have daughters, so I've seen it no less than a dozen times and can recite most of the lines by heart. Flynn Rider is a man who dreams of being happy on a deserted island surrounded by, as the song he sings states, "enormous piles of money." Flynn's dream is to be rich and alone. It is a dream that is self-centered and lame. In other words, it stinks.

If you don't want to pursue a dream that stinks, you need to test your dream. You test your dream by holding it to a standard. If your dream—let's get this out of the way right now—includes things that the Bible describes as sin or that lead others to sin, this is not a God-given dream. It is a stinky, flesh-driven fantasy that needs to be thrown out. There is a big difference between a dream and a fantasy.

Here's another standard you can use to sniff out a stinker. If your dream is to more or less live someone else's life and walk in *their* calling—even if that person is Christian—this too is a fantasy that will leave you disappointed and burned. (We'll dive deeper into this issue later.)

Once you've ruled out the obvious stinkers, your dream needs to meet a few more standards. Your specific standards may ebb and flow a bit, but for me, these are the big three I always use. Ultimately, I believe your dream needs to produce three kinds of fruit:

1. God's name is being glorified.
2. You are walking in your giftings with joy.
3. The darkness of the world is being rolled back.

The next standard—the one I've learned from experience—has to do with the *specificity* of your dream. Your dream should be specific but not *too* specific. In other words, there needs to be some flexibility and room for your dream to take shape in ways you can't yet imagine. Without that, your dream may not exactly stink, but it could be stunted.

I've seen this happen many times, especially when a dream arises from something we see and admire in someone else's calling. For example, you might follow people you admire on social media and begin to fashion a dream with a specific outcome, one that looks just like theirs. Instead of following wherever your dream may take you, you begin to think you need to produce an album or write a book or lead a movement. Nothing is wrong with any of those things, but if your dream is too narrow, too specific, it can produce a rigidness in you that will hinder the beautiful and messy process of discovering more of God's deeper dream for you. If your dream is too specific and your approach too rigid, you risk missing the beautiful redirections God wants you to walk in.

Lastly, and this is key for me, is your dream too small? Many of us become satisfied with dreams that are only as far as our hand can reach. We allow the "realistic" voices of the world to drown out the big, audacious dreams reverberating in our hearts. When your dream extends beyond your natural ability to accomplish it, you know you are in the territory of a God-sized dream. The gap between what you can accomplish and God's dream for your life, is an opportunity for faith. The dreamer who dreams big dreams will continually be drawn to their knees in prayer. If a dream brings equal part excitement and trepidation about how it will be accomplished, you are on the right track!

I love the way Mark Batterson says it in his book *The Circle Maker*. He writes, "Nothing honors God more than a big dream that is way beyond our ability to accomplish it. Why? Because there is no way we can take credit for it. And nothing is better for our spiritual development than a big dream because it keeps us on our knees in raw dependence on God."[1]

So take the time you need to run your dreams through these standards:

1. *Will your dream result in more glory for God, enable you to walk in your giftings with joy, and roll back the darkness in some way?* In other words, will it help you love God more? Will it bring out the best in you and your giftings? Will it make the world a better place?

2. *How specific is your dream?* Is there room for God to shape your dream? Are you flexible and willing to follow any beautiful redirections God may throw your way?
3. *Is your dream too small? Are you dreaming beyond your capacity? Is it something that fills you with equal parts excitement and trepidation? Then you are probably on the right track.*

These aren't theoretical questions; they're practical ones. So take them seriously. Grab a piece of paper—don't worry, I'll wait—and write down your dream. Get it in black and white in front of your eyes and then write whatever comes to mind in response to the questions above. In what ways does your dream meet, or fail to meet, these two standards?

Now run it through the most important filter—the Holy Spirit. Romans 12:2 (ESV) says to let the spirit of God transform us and renew our minds *so that* "by testing you may discern what is the will of God." So bring your dream before the God who promises that discernment. Ask him, *God, is this a dream from you, or is it my own fantasy?* Repeat this process more than once if you need to.

And if you're in a transition time or a confusing season in life and you're still seeking out your dream, that's okay too! There's no rush. Just write down the first thing you can think of that gives you excitement for the future. Maybe it's starting your own business or starting a blog. Maybe it's writing a book or starting a church. Pray and ask for insight. Let your mind wander to the beautiful what-if portions of your mind, then *write something down.*

Writing it down is vital. A recent study found that you are 42 percent more likely to accomplish a goal that is written down than if you just leave it in your head.[2] So take the extra two minutes to write it on a piece of paper or a journal, something you can reference along your journey, something you can come back to or edit as you pursue your dream.

Once you feel as though you have clarity and a green light from God, and you've written down your dream, you're ready to start laying the groundwork, a process that begins with preparation.

PREPARE TO BE PREPARED

There are seasons when I travel a lot. Any kind of travel has its share of challenges, but I travel mostly in a bus—one I share with twelve other people. For weeks. I sleep in a bunk about the size of a coffin, which is what it feels like I may soon be in when our bus driver hits the rumble strips in the middle of the night. A bus is an environment with *no* personal space. Those of us who live on the bus eat all our meals in public. We wear our pajamas in front of strangers. We brush our teeth with an audience. It's twenty-four-seven, nonstop people. As an introvert, to say it's a challenge would be an understatement. But it gets hard when I can't even shower without fear of someone walking in on me.

Our concert venues are mostly basketball arenas, which means our dressing rooms are locker rooms—one large room for men and one large room for women. And there are no private stalls in a locker room shower—it's a large room with multiple shower heads. If you grew up playing sports in high school— which I certainly did *not*—this may seem normal to you. But to me it is far from normal. What's normal is to shower in private, thank you very much.

After several unfortunate incidents of, ahem, exposure, I realized that one thing, and one thing only, would enable me to shower without people getting a thorough view of . . . me. *Preparation.*

If I walk into that shower completely prepared, I can get in and out in two minutes flat. But I have to have everything in place. One false step, and I could end up a peep show. So in case you ever expect to find yourself in a similar situation, here is my go-to preparation list on how to shower in a locker room without giving the world an all-access pass to your birthday suit.

1. *Bring your entire outfit.* If you forget your pants or a clean pair of underwear, you'll be in trouble once the shower starts. So bring it all.
2. *Bring a towel.* Now, in a pinch you can dry off with your dirty clothes, but that seems to negate the shower you just took.
3. *Bring a fold-up chair.* Most times, one is in the dressing room. This will enable you to set your towel and clean clothes on a dry surface.
4. *Bring soap and shampoo.* If you successfully execute steps one through three and begin your shower but then realize you forgot your soap and shampoo, you have failed in the most critical step of the shower process—*to get clean.* Now you must begin all over.

Follow these four simple steps, and you'll dramatically increase the odds of avoiding an awkward exposure moment.

You're welcome.

Preparation. It's key for private showering and for the dreaming process.

One of the best ways to prepare for your dreams is to learn from the lives of other dreamers. The Bible is full of dreamers—people God chose to walk in callings greater than they had ever imagined for themselves. But God needed to help them develop a foundation before they could realize the dreams he had for them. He had to create circumstances in their lives that would prepare them for the road ahead. God created seasons in their lives to refine them, but they needed to partner with him and engage those circumstances to build a strong foundation. God created the context for foundation-building, but the dreamer had to say yes to the call—despite the circumstance. Ultimately, they needed heart-level development, the kind that usually comes only through hardship, so they could handle the bigger challenges they would face along the way.

One of my favorite dreamers in the Bible was a man who had literal dreams from God. That man was Joseph.

Let's take his story from the top.

Now Israel loved Joseph more than any of his other sons, because he had been born to him in his old age; and he made an ornate robe for him. When his brothers saw that their father loved him more than any of them, they hated him and could not speak a kind word to him.

Joseph had a dream, and when he told it to his brothers, they hated him all the more. He said to them, "Listen to this dream I had: We were binding sheaves of grain out in the field when suddenly my sheaf rose and stood upright, while your sheaves gathered around mine and bowed down to it."

His brothers said to him, "Do you intend to reign over us? Will you actually rule us?" And they hated him all the more because of his dream and what he had said.

Then he had another dream, and he told it to his brothers. "Listen," he said, "I had another dream, and this time the sun and moon and eleven stars were bowing down to me."

When he told his father as well as his brothers, his father rebuked him and said, "What is this dream you had? Will your mother and I and your brothers actually come and bow down to the ground before you?" His brothers were jealous of him, but his father kept the matter in mind. (Genesis 37:3–11)

Now, Joseph is clearly not winning any popularity contests. He is Dad's favorite, so a complicated family dynamic is going on. When he naively shares his audacious dreams, he doesn't get the reaction he probably hoped for. But for now, let's hone in on one thing: Joseph's dream was macro, not micro.

Joseph gets the general sense that he will be a man of great influence. He gets the general sense that realizing his dream will trump cultural norms, that he will somehow lead his family despite being the second-to-youngest child rather than the oldest. He gets the general sense that God is telling him, "Joseph, I have created you for more."

But notice what God *doesn't* tell Joseph. He doesn't tell him *how* he will get there. He doesn't tell him *how long* it will take to get there or even *what* he will be doing when he does get there. God gives him the general, not the specific.

That sounds fine for Joseph because we already know the story has a happy ending. But what is it we tend to stress about when God gives us a big dream? It's the details, right? We want the specifics, the things our limited human minds consider the basic facts we need to know. *What am I doing with my life, God? How long will it take to realize these dreams you've given me? What does my current season have to do with the passions in my heart for something greater?*

Or maybe your dream came complete with specifics. You are destined to be doctor or a preacher or a business owner. You've known it since you were five and have walked out your plan to a T without any hiccups. Good for you! You can probably put this book down now. Thanks for spending some time with us today.

The rest of us have a journey more like Joseph's. Joseph gets a message that says, "You will be a man of great influence," whereupon his life immediately plunges into the proverbial toilet. For a long time. And by long, I mean thirteen years, with at least two of those years spent in prison for a crime he didn't commit. When God gave Joseph a dream, he conveniently left those parts out. He also didn't tell him about all the wisdom he'd gain in those foundation-building years. Or how the hardships he endured would prepare him to take on the challenges of his calling. Instead, God was with Joseph, using his challenges to prepare him, because once his dream came to fruition, Joseph would face even greater challenges.

That's the thing with God. Most of the time, the reward for conquering challenges isn't a cushier assignment but an even greater challenge. You have been warned!

If you are in a season of preparation and foundation-building, then you are likely facing great challenges. Your job isn't what you'd hoped. Your friends and family don't understand what you are called to. You are so busy with work or kids that you can't imagine finding time to eat, let alone dream. Whatever the challenges may be, don't worry! Challenges—even a lack of free time—by themselves are not a sign that you should give up on your dream. The opposite is more likely true. If you've got challenges, you're in good company. Take it from Joseph: the challenges of the dreamer are many and difficult, but they can be overcome. And it's in that very process of overcoming that God prepares you and builds your foundation. So don't stress about not knowing the specifics. Choose instead to trust that God is with you just as he was with Joseph and that he is at work—in you as well as in your circumstances.

Whatever challenge you are facing, anchor your trust back on the powerful, purposeful, and miraculous nature of the Dream Giver. Engage your current circumstances with the anticipation of how God will use this season to prepare you for what's ahead. That's how you begin to lay the groundwork for what is to come. And most of this groundwork is identity-centered, so get ready to dive deep. Identity is vital because what you believe about God and yourself will be either your greatest asset or your greatest liability as you pursue your calling.

CHAPTER 3

CREATIVE GENIUSES

I was the kid who always had his head in the clouds.

I could spend hours inventing intricate and outlandish imaginary worlds and drawing pictures or writing stories about them. Sometimes I dreamed up worlds filled with dinosaurs or space travel. Other times I imagined that I was treasure hunting in a far-off country or that I was a superhero who could fly. The "real" world was boring and limiting, but in my head, *anything* was possible.

This ability to get lost in an imaginary world wasn't a problem until I took up T-ball. Natural athlete that I was not, I was usually assigned to outfield, which meant I got very little action. Most of the time, I sat down and played with blades of grass or stared at the clouds—that is, until my coach's yelling broke through my introvert stupor. "Come on, Romeo, hustle!" You might think that meant a batter had hit the ball my way, but most of the time it meant I needed to get into the dugout. The inning was over, and now we were on offense. *Offense? Oh yeah. Hitting the ball.*

When it was my turn at bat, I'd swing a couple of times and eventually hit the ball. So far, so good. But then my mind would wander again. *Where is the ball going? I wonder who's gonna catch it.*

What was that sound? Was that a car accident? Or maybe construction is going on somewhere. . . .

Meanwhile, my coach would have to chase me to first base to make sure I didn't forget to run.

Yep, that was me. A regular six-year-old jock.

CLAIM YOUR IDENTITY

Imagination. Dreaming. Curiosity. Wondering.

This is the natural state for most children. We don't start off in life consumed with thoughts about our schedule or productivity. Instead, we spend hours making a mud pit in the yard. Or jumping up and down with excitement over filling jars with water and food coloring so we can pretend that they are some sort of magic potion—which happens to be what my kids are doing as I write this.

None of this struck us as a waste of time. None of this induced guilt that we should be doing something "better" with our lives. We *allowed* ourselves the emotional space to create for the sake of creating. We *allowed* ourselves to dream. We *allowed* ourselves to spend *time* on dreams. And the ability to dream was as easy as waking up in the morning.

So what happened between childhood and now?

Disappointment, heartbreak, and rejection. That's a lot for the heart of a little dreamer to bear. And so, in response to all this pain, you distanced yourself from anything that might lead to more disappointment, heartbreak, or rejection. Dreams and imagination start to feel risky for a wounded heart, and so you either calloused yourself or hid yourself to avoid the risks.

The older you get, the more you need to fight to keep the dreamer in you alive. The more you need to actively create space and habits to keep your eyes looking to the horizon and imagining a new future. The more you need to claim your identity as a creative *genius*.

Yes. You read that right. No, I'm not joking. You need to dive headlong into the brilliant and unique creativity that you alone bring to the world. It's the foundation of your dream.

To go after our dreams with full confidence, we need to get back to that place we knew so well in childhood—that place of imagination, dreaming, curiosity, and wondering. We do that by first dismantling a warped idea we bought into somewhere along the way, and one we still hear all the time because it's so pervasive. The warped idea is this: *some people are just born creative, and the rest of us aren't.* It's a warped idea because it confuses creativity and the ability to dream with a personality type. Some people just "have it," and other people—namely, you—not so much.

Allow me to call that idea what it is: a big, fat lie.

Here's the truth: there is no such thing as an *un*creative person.

Now, if you don't consider yourself creative and you're thinking of skipping this chapter, hear me out. I want you to consider that the word *creative* has largely been misused in our culture. Notice that I didn't say "artistic," I said *creative*. There is a difference.

Creativity is a human trait—one built right into our DNA. It's what enables us to solve problems, have unique perspectives, and make meaning in our lives. That's why creativity is part of our identity. It's vital for life. The problem is that many of us have confused *creative* with *artistic*. And not only artistic but the stereotype of an "artsy" person. The mom who posts her brilliant crafts to Pinterest or has carefully curated photos of their kids on Instagram. The couple whose house looks like Joanna Gaines designed it. The guy who wears acetate glasses, has a bushy beard, and probably works for an architect firm or branding agency. Many of us have seen the *super* "creative" people in our lives as . . . well . . . a bit off. People who burn incense and spend five hours a day in coffeehouses just . . . *thinking*. They wear tie-dye, live in VW vans, and use crystals—quite ineffectively—for deodorant. But I digress . . .

I understand where this comes from. When the artistic gets confused with the creative, creativity can feel weird and abstract, like a mystical and intangible force that applies only to a rare few. Leonardo da Vinci. Maya Angelou. Mozart. Einstein. Steve Jobs. Annie Leibovitz. Or, self-proclaimed creative genius, Kanye West. We hear their stories and are amazed by what they have accomplished. Surely these are the true creative geniuses of the world, right?

Yes, these are amazing individuals, but we must also recognize their humanity. It's almost as if we believe they aren't human—that they haven't experienced disappointment, rejection, setbacks. But they do have flaws and have made mistakes. Leonardo da Vinci was born illegitimate. Maya Angelou was abused and came from a home fraught with brokenness and murder. Mozart struggled financially for most of his life and died at age thirty-five. Einstein struggled profoundly in school, and his father died seeing his son only as a failure. Steve Jobs got kicked out of Apple—the company he launched—and started another company that crashed and burned. Annie Leibovitz almost went bankrupt at the height of her career. And Kanye . . . well Kanye's struggles are plain for all to see. You can probably see where I'm going with this. Ultimately, their stories look a lot like, well, our stories.

But through the rosy lens of history, we gloss over all their failures and struggles. It's as though we believe that these people are superhuman, so their stories must be superhuman—or at least something more extraordinary than our own. I mean, we aren't extraordinary. We're just normal people, not creative geniuses, right?

Here's the thing. There is no such thing as a "normal" person. *You* are not a normal person. You are unique and creative. You may not change global history or be studied in schools one day, but you are far from ordinary.

If you're a graphic designer, a worship leader, or a photographer, that may not be such a challenging idea to accept, because creativity is already a high value for you. But if you're an engineer or a CPA or a computer programmer, I'm guessing you could be thinking something like, *Ryan, I'm up to my eyeballs in calculations, Excel spreadsheets, or code. There is nothing creative about that!*

Sure, your calculations, spreadsheets, or code may not move people to tears—although, they might!—but they represent the *work* you do. Every job carries the potential for you to shine, to approach even the most mundane tasks with fresh eyes and a desire to make them better, to use your imagination or original ideas in one-of-a-kind ways.

This is creativity at its best—you being you. You are creative when you leverage your unique gifts and perspectives to maximize whatever task you undertake.

Only you carry the unique ability to be *you*. There is nobody like you. There is nobody who thinks like you. Or solves problems like you. God has created you to be *you*. And by definition, that makes you creative.

But if you're the scientific type and you need more evidence, I have some of that for you too.

✧ ✧

Biologists tell us that we are born with forty-six chromosomes—
twenty-three from our father and twenty-three from our mother.
At conception, the chromosomes we got from our father line
up with the chromosomes we got from our mother, and they
recombine to make a unique combination. As if this weren't
complicated enough, a process called *recombination* takes place.
These chromosomes swap DNA with one another creating unique
mutations. Now, there are nearly three billion DNA base pairs,
which means that the recombination process can get complex.

Sandeep Venkataram, a biologist from Stanford, describes
it this way:

> From a pure information theory perspective, there are tens
> of millions of cataloged mutations across all human popula-
> tions. A few million of these are common, . . . and the rest are
> rare. Just considering say the 1 million common mutations,
> just by sampling on average you will get the rare version
> 10,000 times and the common version 990,000 times. So
> the probability that two different people have the same
> set of mutations, just in this set of common mutations, is
> $0.99^{990,000} \times 0.01^{10,000}$ which is an astronomically tiny num-
> ber. You have a better shot of randomly choosing the same
> atom in the known universe twice than you do of having two
> different people getting the same set of mutations twice.[1]

I had to read that eight times before it sunk in. And my brain
still hurts a little. But this is the point: the probability of you
having the same genetic code as anyone else on earth—even

all the people who ever lived throughout history—is effectively zero. From the very moment of your conception, you were hard-wired to be unique—to see the world in ways no one else does. And there's more.

Take into account the uniqueness of your upbringing, including the culture you live in and the life lessons you've learned through your parents, friends, and teachers. All of these—whether good, bad, or ugly—are outside influences that shape the internal you. Again, all of it unique to you. And the same thing is true of the current relationships and circumstances that continue to impact you in dynamic ways.

Are you starting to grasp how insanely complex the system is that goes into making you *you*? I can barely wrap my head around it. But God not only understands it, he masterminded it—*all of it*. He created the mind-blowing complexity that created a one-of-a-kind you. And he took all of it into account when he gave you a dream and a calling.

You are creative because you were created in the image of an incredibly creative God. You are a creator just as God is the Creator. And your creativity is unlike anyone else on earth. You are an unrepeatable child of God. There never has been and never will be anyone else like you. That's your identity in God. It's also why the greatest pursuit of your life is to better understand the character of God—the more amazed you are by the Dream Giver, the better you'll understand the uniqueness of your calling. You'll not only understand it but be awed by it to the point of seeing your own story, gifts, and calling with wonder and gratitude.

Why is this so important? Because if you don't know who you are—especially in relationship to God—all kinds of other forces in the world will try to define you in lesser and limiting ways.

IDENTITY ANCHORS

In the absence of an identity based on what God says about you, you will tether yourself to something else. Something temporary. Something that will leave a gaping hole in your heart when it leaves.

I like to call these *identity anchors*. Identity anchors are anything in which we place a significant amount of our identity. It's the thing we filter all our self-talk around. This can be your profession or your behavior. This can be things we feel are inherited from our parents or our culture. Now, *unhealthy* identity anchors are anything that is not anchored to the immovable and unique identity that God places on you. They are anchors into the temporal things of this world that can change on a dime.

One of the most common identity anchors is your profession. Our most natural go-to is to weave what we do into who we are. And the world around us loves to identify you based on your profession, skills, or education. You are an architect, so you hang out with other architects and talk architect things. But what happens when you are laid off and can't get another architect job? You no longer know how to be you anymore because your identity got laid off too.

You can also easily anchor your identity to your family. Your dad was angry. His dad was angry. And anger so intertwined with your family identity and experience that it's hard to imagine who you are without it.

Or maybe your issue is your sexual identity or behavior. The world wants to confuse what you do or don't do sexually with who you are so that you are not fully *you* anymore. Instead, you are reduced to *promiscuous you*, or *celibate you*, or *gay you*, or *straight you*, or *transgender you*. And the expectation is that every other aspect of your life must be subject to that one aspect of what you do.

All these forces in the world want to anchor your identity to a label, a label you take on, a label that finishes this sentence, "I'm just a . . ." Pastor. Engineer. Secretary. Bad business person. Emotional person. Angry person. Adulterer. Fool with my money. Whatever label the world has slapped on your back, the enemy will use it to distort your identity and to distract you as much as possible from becoming the true you who God sees.

A label is not an identity. It is a forgery of your true identity. And sooner or later, it will fail you.

So how do we combat these unhealthy identity anchors? How can we continually be anchoring back to something more solid and sure?

This begins with the simple but loaded question: Who does God say you are?

HOW YOU'RE SEEN

The Bible is full of what I call *global* identity anchors. These are general, metaphorical identities found in Scripture. These anchors are literally *everywhere* in the Bible. I've often found little tidbits of them throughout Scripture, and they are great places to start. Here are a few among countless to dive into.

- You are *a child* of God. 1 John 3 reminds us that you are his child. You are not just a subject in his vast, faceless army. You are his kid. You are one of his very own.

- You are a temple of the Holy Spirit. The end of 1 Corinthians 6 reminds us that we were purchased with the price of Jesus's sacrifice on the cross. Because of that, our bodies are now the temple where God resides. You are a vessel that carries the presence of God wherever you go. What an amazing honor!

- If you want a verse with a condensed dose of healthy biblical identity, 1 Peter 2:9 is one of the best places to go. It says, "You are a chosen people, a royal priesthood, a holy nation, God's special possession."

Let those sink in. You were chosen by God. Handpicked. You are a priest. You connect God and people together. You are a special possession. You belong to him, and he is so proud of you.

These are all universal, biblical identity anchors. They are vital. To know what God says about you is so important, and it is the best place to start reorienting misplaced identity anchors. But we have to move these concepts from head to heart. What God thinks about you is foundational, but how you see yourself is just as important.

HOW YOU SEE YOURSELF

In Numbers 13 we see Moses trying to lead the people of God into the promised land. This was land that God had literally *promised* to give them. They had just seen God destroy the vast and powerful army of Pharaoh by miraculously crushing them between a parted sea. They had already come so far and were about to enter into the promise of God. They are so close. By Numbers 13 they are sending spies into the land to check it out. But then something happens. Misplaced identity anchors take over. When they come back from spying on the land, everything begins to unravel.

> They gave Moses this account: "We went into the land to which you sent us, and it does flow with milk and honey! Here is its fruit. But the people who live there are powerful, and the cities are fortified and very large. We even saw descendants of Anak there . . . .
>
> Then Caleb silenced the people before Moses and said, "We should go up and take possession of the land, for we can certainly do it."
>
> But the men who had gone up with him said, "We can't attack those people; they are stronger than we are. . . . The land we explored devours those living in it. All the people we saw there are of great size. We saw the Nephilim there (the descendants of Anak come from the Nephilim). We seemed like grasshoppers in our own eyes, and we looked the same to them." (Numbers 13:27–28, 30–33)

Did you catch that? "We seemed like grasshoppers *in our own eyes* . . ." They had a perception of themselves that was not in line with the power of God. They had an identity anchored only to their own physical ability.

And before we chastise them for not remembering the power of God, we need to look in the mirror.

This is the point where you need to do work with the Holy Spirit. This is where hearing from God in prayer is so vital. Spend less time talking to God and more time listening. He will give you identity that isn't just rooted in the global truth found in

Scripture but is also something intimate and just for you. And through that, we will begin to see ourselves not as grasshoppers but as powerful children of God. We will begin to see the unique and creative version of ourselves that God sees.

CREATIVE IDENTITY

Here is the point in all of this: when it comes to realizing your dreams, it's not *what* you will be doing but *who* God says you are that matters most. I want you to read one more bit of Scripture before we move on from identity. This is not just a fact about who you are; it gives you an intimate view of God's heart toward you, his desire and purpose he carried while creating you. I want you to take a deep breath and read this out loud over yourself. These words were originally written by King David as a prayer, so don't just read them—pray them.

> You formed my innermost being, shaping my delicate inside
> and my intricate outside,
> and wove them all together in my mother's womb.
> I thank you, God, for making me so mysteriously complex!
> Everything you do is marvelously breathtaking.
> It simply amazes me to think about it!
> How thoroughly you know me, Lord!
> You even formed every bone in my body
> when you created me in the secret place,
> carefully, skillfully shaping me from nothing to something.
> You saw who you created me to be before I became me!
> Before I'd ever seen the light of day,

the number of days you planned for me
were already recorded in your book.
Every single moment you are thinking of me!
How precious and wonderful to consider
that you cherish me constantly in your every thought!
O God, your desires toward me are more
than the grains of sand on every shore!
When I awake each morning, you're still with me.
    (Psalm 139:13–18 TPT)

Good, right? Take another deep breath if you need to. Let the words wash over you. This is a beautiful and profound glimpse into who you are, a glimpse into the unwarped, unpolluted view of how God sees you. He made you carefully and purposefully. He thinks about you. He *wants* to be with you. This is all part of the foundation of your true and anchored identity.

A healthy identity is an identity that nobody can steal from you. When God tells you who you are and you take him at his word, no discouragement will dissuade you. No challenge will overtake you. No other voices will be able to tell you who you are. Finding true identity in your Creator brings unprecedented freedom and power.

A healthy identity begins with anchoring to the truth of knowing you were created by God and that God never makes mistakes with his creations. It is in knowing you are created in the image of the Creator that you unleash more creativity in your life, because creativity is the fruit of understanding your true identity. Creativity—at its core—is conquering fear so you can discover more of your God-given potential. It's the process of finding out what makes you *you* and finding the freedom to keep exploring how God made you. That's when you begin to walk through life with your eyes open to the creativity already inside you and those around you.

Creativity is part of the foundational identity of the dreamer. You will never dive into the new, unique dream until you know your identity is found in God and God alone.

Now, you may be thinking, "Ryan, to call me creative is one thing, but a *creative genius*? Don't creative geniuses make history? Aren't they earth-shaking and culture-altering?"

My answer to all those questions is *yes*.

✧ ✧

My three kids make some incredible art, some of the most moving and beautiful art I've ever seen. Most times, it's comical and care-free. But at times it's gut-wrenching, especially when I'm about to go out of town and they draw or paint something to tell me how much they'll miss me. I have never experienced any other art that comes close to packing that kind of emotional punch.

Which is why I consider my kids *creative geniuses*.

I imagine you may be skeptical. I mean, they all are currently under the age of ten. And I concede that no one would consider their art professional or even realistic. Their artistic style is more of a Picasso-like abstraction of real life. For example, not all the people in their drawings have arms or feet. And our dog? Well, she is often depicted as a blob with four sticks coming out of her belly.

So what makes my kids creative geniuses?

Allow me to quote the all-knowing Google, which defines a genius as "a person who is exceptionally intelligent or creative, either generally or in some particular respect." I love that phrase *exceptionally intelligent or creative*. Not ordinary, but extraordinary. A genius is someone greater than all the "normal people" out there.

But remember, none of us is *normal*. And I'm guessing you already know that because you've felt it. Have you ever felt as if you're an outsider? As though you don't fit in? As if there is an in-crowd and you're not part of it?

I feel this way all the time. As though I don't fit. As if I'm the square peg that doesn't fit the round hole of whatever the group may be, especially when it's a big group. In a crowd it seems as if everyone has someone to talk to except me, as if the other people in the room are surrounded by a force field and I have to find some way to bust through it to join a conversation. If I do get lucky enough to get in, I blow it with awkward comments. I stutteringly bring up a movie I loved, and suddenly I can't remember the title. I trip over my words even when I ask something simple like, "What did you do today?" That's a pretty simple sentence, one I should have been able to master after a few decades on planet earth. But instead it comes out as, "When did you today?" or "Did you . . . do . . . stuff . . . today?" or my personal favorite, "Wahdoyoudoaday?" A small butchering of the English language inevitably exits my mouth, I turn red, smack my forehead (on the inside), say, "*Idiot!*" (hopefully also on the inside), and walk away with my tail between my legs.

Even if I'm alone in this particular struggle, I believe we all feel outside the in-crowd at some point. But what if this outsider feeling is a marker of something beautiful and true? What if this alone feeling leads to an extraordinary revelation of identity that helps us to see ourselves through the lens of a creative and loving Father?

I know being on the outside of the in-crowd certainly doesn't feel beautiful. But I think it could be a reflection of the beautiful truth that we aren't like anyone else—that we are truly one-of-a-kind creations. This can either lead us to feel isolated and lonely or it can lead us to feel free—free to be the person God designed us to be.

You may feel as though nobody truly understands you. And guess what? You're right. No human being on earth truly understands what is going on between your ears. Only one being in the universe can fully understand you, and that is the One who made you.

God doesn't compare you to anyone. He doesn't wish you were something different or someone else. How can you be normal? How can you be boring or mundane? *God made you.* He made you on purpose. He made you unique—different from every other person. You aren't ordinary. You are *extraordinary*. The more you believe and embrace this truth, the more your own creative genius will come alive and explode out of you. This is the kind of genius who alters history. This is the kind of genius who shifts culture. It's the genius who is unequivocally themselves.

Here's how Jesus puts it: "It's who you are and the way you live that count before God. Your worship must engage your spirit in the pursuit of truth. That's the kind of people the Father is out looking for: those who are simply and honestly *themselves* before him in their worship" (John 4:23–24 MSG).

Did you catch that? *God is looking for those who are simply and honestly themselves.* I hope that blows your mind as much as it does mine. I hope it sets you free. I hope it helps to embrace your creative genius.

Being who you are before God takes practice, a whole lifetime of it for most of us. But it's a pursuit that will always lead to more life. More freedom. And more creativity pouring out of you.

You are a creative genius. There is no such thing as an uncreative person.

If you believe that your creativity—your unique ideas, perspectives, and identity—comes from being handcrafted by a creative and loving God, then you have a sure foundation from which to pursue your dreams. And you will run toward them without even considering that there might be such a thing as a plan B. You will live with confidence that the dreams and visions within you are from the same God that parted the Red Sea in Exodus. You will see yourself not as a grasshopper but as a giant walking into your own *promised* land.

But for this sort of confidence, we have to put an identity anchor into an idea that goes back to creation.

SUBDUE

I've learned a lot from other dreamers, and one of my favorites is Apple founder Steve Jobs. I especially love the empowering way he talked about making a difference in the world:

> When you grow up you tend to get told that the world is the way it is and your life is just to live your life inside the world. Try not to bash into the walls too much. Try to have a nice family life, have fun, save a little money. That's a very limited life. Life can be much broader once you discover one simple fact—everything around you that you call life was made up by people that were no smarter than you. And you

can change it, you can influence it . . . Once you learn that, you'll never be the same again.[2]

It's easy to say something like this, but Steve Jobs did it—pursuing his dreams and visions literally changed the world. Through Apple, we shifted to digital music, and we got iPhones that led to things such as Uber and Instagram. These inventions changed our lives and the world around us. We can bring digital Bibles into any closed country now. Technologies that would have felt magical or miraculous just a few decades ago are now practically ho-hum routine.

Steve Jobs tapped into a source of freedom and authority that existed long before he ever walked the planet, and that's what enabled him to realize his vision. Jobs's freedom and authority were given to him by his Creator. The same freedom and authority are also given to us by our Creator. And we have documentation! It happened in the first chapter of our story.

> Then God said, "Let us make mankind in our image, in our likeness, so that they may rule over the fish in the sea and the birds in the sky, over the livestock and all the wild animals, and over all the creatures that move along the ground."

> So God created mankind in his own image,
>   in the image of God he created them;
>   male and female he created them.

> God blessed them and said to them, "Be fruitful and increase in number; fill the earth and subdue it. Rule over

the fish in the sea and the birds in the sky and over every living creature that moves on the ground." . . .

Now the LORD God had formed out of the ground all the wild animals and all the birds in the sky. He brought them to the man to see what he would name them; and whatever the man called each living creature, that was its name. So the man gave names to all the livestock, the birds in the sky and all the wild animals. (Genesis 1:26–28; 2:19–20)

In Genesis 1, God gave human beings something of great power and significance. That thing is dominion. God charged humankind with the responsibility to subdue the earth. That means to bring order to chaos, to control the seemingly uncontrollable, to create an environment in which every living thing could flourish. This is a big charge. A grand and royal calling. And one that applies to you and me as much as it did to Adam and Eve.

God gave a human being the authority to name all the animals on earth, to be fruitful, to rule over creatures and creation. Authority is license to change things, and change is creative innovation. God calls you and me to exercise that same authority by pursuing our dreams—that's part of how we make a difference in the world. But what happens when we take a pass on that authority? When we give up because we feel as though something in our lives can never change or that our circumstances can never be different? I'll tell you what happens: we will never take the risk to innovate and pursue anything new. That is the death of dreams.

But that's not going to happen to *our* dreams. Not today, Satan. God has given us authority and charged us to subdue the seemingly unsubduable—and that's what we're going to do.

We are going to unleash our creative genius on the world around us and watch it change in ways we never imagined.

But how do we do this? What does subduing mean for you and me today? Especially if we feel as though we're stuck in a season of life with few options and limited resources?

To access our power and authority—to subdue—we must understand God's power and authority.

We need to know the character of the Dream Giver.

CHAPTER 4

THE DREAM GIVER

My nine-year-old son Toby is confident.

He is a classic firstborn with a strong sense of his own capabilities. He is boisterous and inquisitive. He loves every sport and has a deep curiosity about science. He loves building things and being around people. But more than all those things, he loves to travel with me on tour.

The traveling crew for the OUTCRY tour typically includes around twelve tour buses, four semis, and a hundred people. We travel every day to a new city for three to four weeks in a row. It's a high-energy, nonstop, go-go-go environment—basically everything Toby loves.

Toby knows how to tour as if he owns the place. He typically brings some sort of wheeled apparatus—a skateboard, scooter, hoverboard, *anything* that makes him go fast—and flies around the arena wearing three all-access passes (because one evidently is not enough). All the security guards quickly learn his name. All the bands quickly get to know the whirlwind that is Toby. And now he has something else that helps him feel extra special on tour. He is the little boy featured on our OUTCRY logo.

Years before I had any idea that we would be taking OUTCRY on the road, I drew up a logo using Toby as my model. I drew him, well, crying out.

He likes being logo-famous, though it seems to have gone to his head somewhat. He sometimes asks questions such as, "How many shirts am I on this year, Daddy?" If he sees an enlargement of the logo somewhere, he is drawn to it as  a moth is to a bright light. He stands and stares at it, his face beaming with pride. Or sometimes while on tour, he likes to "go shopping." Now, this is not him actually buying anything. Toby's version of shopping consists of him going to our merch table and getting free stuff. He rolls up to the table with a pensive look on his face and says, "Can I have that hat . . . and that shirt? In a small, please."

One day Toby arrived at the merch table when Mike, our merch guy, wasn't on duty. Mike knows who Toby is and hooks him up. But on this day, Mike wasn't behind the table, and in his place were two college girls who were volunteering. But that didn't faze Toby. With full confidence, he said, "Can I get a hat and a small shirt?"

The girls—not knowing Toby's pedigree—looked at him sympathetically and responded, "Sorry, little boy. We aren't allowed to give this stuff away. Go find your daddy and ask him if he can come buy it for you."

Toby, who had never before been denied a perk, was undaunted. "Oh, I'm sorry," he said. "Maybe you don't know, but that's me on that shirt. See that kid yelling into that megaphone? That's me. And my dad basically runs this place. So can you please get a hat and a small shirt for me?"

After giving one another quizzical looks, the girls shrugged and gave him the merch! A little kid basically peer-pressured two college students more than twice his age to give him free stuff! Oh, Toby.

Now, to clarify, I wasn't there. I heard this story secondhand. And had I been there, I would have said, "Buddy, that's not how we act. Jesus said the last would be first and the first would be last . . ." (Insert embarrassed-dad lecture here.)

When I got home from tour, I shared the story with my friend Nick. Nick is a guy with a lot of godly insight, and he made a comment that blew me away.

"That's actually a beautiful story," he said.

To which I responded incredulously, "How so?"

"Toby knows who his dad is," Nick said. "He walks around on that tour knowing the authority of his father. Imagine if we all did that."

Boom.

Let that one sink in a minute.

What if you went through life knowing who your Dad is? Not your earthly dad. I'm talking about the Dad who created you. The One who knit you together, who has good plans for you, who believes in your dream more than you do.

If you're dreaming about something that seems impossible, how would it impact your confidence if you knew that God's realm is in the impossible. He lives there. Your Dad doesn't get scared or doubt, and he doesn't second-guess your calling. When you know that your Dad dwells in the realm of the impossible, those "impossible" obstacles between you and your dreams start to look a lot smaller.

When it comes to chasing your dreams, knowing who your Dad is changes everything.

THE DREAM GIVER'S ATTRIBUTES

One of the best ways to learn more about God's character is to immerse ourselves in his written Word. The Bible is the stories of God, inspired by God, to bring glory to God. When we read the stories of how God loved and led and cared for his people, we discover his attributes. An attribute is a quality that is inherent, which means it is permanent and unchanging. While God's actions are as creative as the circumstances demand, God's character—his attributes—are constant.

To learn more about God's character, we're going to explore three of his attributes—the kind of attributes that will give you confidence when you step out into the calling and dreams he has for your life. Each section begins with two or three verses that anchor that attribute in Scripture. Hold tightly to these truths, and they will be your life raft when you hit treacherous waters on the journey to fulfill his purpose for your life.

God Dwells in the Impossible

When I look at the night sky and see the work of your
     fingers—
          the moon and the stars you set in place—
what are mere mortals that you should think about them,
          human beings that you should care for them?
          (Psalm 8:3–4 NLT)

Ah, Lord GOD! It is you who have made the heavens and the earth by your great power and by your outstretched arm! Nothing is too hard for you. (Jeremiah 32:17 ESV)

We are created in the image of God, but he is something wholly other than we are. He created everything we see and everything we can't see. He created the universe we live in. He planned and imagined every detail. Nothing escaped his creativity and purpose. And for this meticulously created universe, he invented rules that govern it. And as the inventor, he is free to break those rules—and often does—whenever he likes. The Psalmist recognizes that the only appropriate response in the face of such beauty and untouchable power is humble awe. When we see ourselves in relation to God's greatness, we realize our appropriate size—small.

Many dreamers need a good dose of humility—the *humble* side of humble awe—when pursuing a big dream. If we aren't careful, we can make our work too important. It's easy to believe we are on the most important mission on earth—because for *us*, it is. But before we become too important in our own eyes, we need to remember how much bigger God is, even bigger than our dreams. Our dreams are important, but they are not bigger than the One who gave them. Neither do they outrank other people's dreams. When all we see is the grandness of our own dream, we might even begin to use those around us to accomplish it. If you don't learn to routinely seek out humility, it may eventually seek you out in the form of humiliating circumstances. Choose the former—daily.

Other dreamers need a good dose of confidence—the *awe* side of humble awe. We look around at all the challenges we face, and our calling becomes a source of fear. We wake up in the middle of the night worrying and wondering how we'll be able to pull it off. That's when we lean into awe and remind ourselves that God dwells in the impossible. We marinate our thoughts in this truth until it becomes a natural part of our thought patterns. God isn't simply able to perform the impossible, he *dwells* in the realm of the impossible. Nothing is too hard for him. Nothing. So whenever we are fearful, we remind ourselves of God's greatness and that he is faithful to fulfill the dreams he gives.

God Is Faithful and Reliable

God is not human, that he should lie,
>   not a human being, that he should change his mind.
Does he speak and then not act?
>   Does he promise and not fulfill? (Numbers 23:19)

I pray with great faith for you, because I'm fully convinced that the One who began this glorious work in you will faithfully continue the process of maturing you and will put his finishing touches to it until the unveiling of our Lord Jesus Christ! (Philippians 1:6 TPT)

He who calls you is faithful; he will surely do it. (1 Thessalonians 5:24 ESV)

The world is moving and shifting. Your life is moving and shifting. Your mood will move and shift. Some days you'll feel great about your calling. You will feel excited and hopeful. But most days you won't. Many times along the way, the barriers around you will look insurmountable. The problems you face will look so daunting you might conclude that the only reasonable response is to give up.

This is normal. It's even to be expected. When you hit a wall and think it's time to give up, run to this attribute of God—he is faithful and reliable. He is committed to you. Even when everything shifts like sand, God is solid ground. Hold on to him. He is faithful to walk you into your calling regardless of your circumstances. He doesn't second-guess his choice in you, so you shouldn't either.

If you've had people in your life who were unfaithful—who walked out on you, lied to you, or abandoned you when you needed them most—it might be difficult to imagine anyone could be worthy of trust. And you are right that human beings are unreliable. But don't put that on God.

God never misleads or taunts the human soul. He is the faithful one. He will never leave you, never lie to you, never abandon you. God is not like unreliable human beings. He is faithful and reliable, a steady rock in a shifting-sand world.

God Is the Source of Unfailing Love

We love because he first loved us. (1 John 4:19)

"I love each of you with the same love that the Father loves me. You must continually let my love nourish your hearts. If you keep my commands, you will live in my love, just as I have kept my Father's commands, for I continually live nourished and empowered by his love. My purpose for telling you these things is so that the joy that I experience will fill your hearts with overflowing gladness!" (John 15:9–11 TPT)

I spent considerable screen time with Mister Rogers as a child. To me, he wasn't just a nerd in a sweater on TV. He was one of the first men who ministered to my heart through his love.

Some people don't know that Fred Rogers was an ordained minister. He went to seminary. And every morning on *Mister Rogers' Neighborhood*, he preached powerful and brave messages to his small viewers. He communicated the love of God to those who are close to Jesus's heart—children. Among many wonderful and profound statements he made about love was this:

> Deep within us—no matter who we are—there lives a feeling of wanting to be lovable, of wanting to be the kind of person that others like to be with. And the greatest thing we can do is to let people know that they are loved and capable of loving. . . . Love and trust, in the space between what's said and what's heard in our life, can make all the difference in this world.

I'm guessing you already know about this attribute of God, but knowing *about* something is not the same thing as *knowing* it. When you know *about* God's love, you have information. But when you *know* God's love, you have God. When you know God's love, you know you are not only loved but lovable. You know the love and acceptance of your Creator. This foundational knowing has the power to fuel you with faith, heal you with grace, and remove your fear and shame.

It's important to know that your Dad dwells in the impossible and that he is faithful and reliable. But if you rely on these attributes without also allowing yourself to know, really know, the grounding revelation of his love, you run the risk of becoming rigid and religious rather than flexible and loving as you work toward your dream.

I want you to read a chunk of the Bible that may be numbingly familiar to you. If it is, you may need to read it several times. Sit in a posture of receiving by allowing your hands to rest in your lap, palms up. Then read it with an open heart, truly seeking a new revelation about the nature of God's love for you.

> Love is *large and* incredibly patient. Love is gentle and consistently kind to all. It refuses to be jealous *when blessing comes to someone else*. Love does not brag about one's achievements nor inflate its own importance. Love does not traffic in shame and disrespect, nor selfishly seek its own honor. Love is not easily irritated or quick to take offense. Love joyfully celebrates honesty and finds no delight in what is wrong. Love is a safe place of shelter, for it never stops believing the best for others. Love never takes failure as defeat, for it never gives up. Love never stops loving. It extends beyond the gift of prophecy, which eventually fades away. It is more enduring than tongues, which will one day fall silent. Love remains long after *words of* knowledge are forgotten. (1 Corinthians 13:4–8 TPT)

In a world full of contradicting and confused notions of love, this passage always provides insight into God's nature and the true meaning of love. We could dive into so much more here, but God's nature is something we will be continually discovering for the rest of our lives. Every day God has a new revelation to give about who he is and what he is like if we keep our eyes open and our attention on him. At some point our discovery of the Dream Giver's nature inevitably leads us to God's promises for the dream receiver.

THE DREAM GIVER'S PROMISES

When we examine the Bible, we learn not only the attributes of God that describe what he is like but also the attributes that describe what God is like *toward* us. Now, this might seem to be a subtle distinction, but follow me on this. When we study God's nature, we learn about who he is—for example, that he is omniscient, omnipotent, and omnipresent. But we can also study God's nature to learn how he relates to us as individuals.

Imagine, for example, the president of the United States. You can study the nature of the president. You can learn about his lineage and past accomplishments. You can examine his personal habits and personality traits. You can discover his work ethic or favorite foods. You can read or compile volumes of information about him. Many authors and commentators do this. They study what can be told by other books or interviews with people who knew him best.

But what if you got a personal invitation to sit with the president himself? What would you learn about him then?

The invitation tells you that Air Force One is waiting at the airport and that you—and you alone—have a meeting set with the president. As you arrive in DC with Secret Service agents flanking you and black SUVs driving you to the most famous house in America, you are overwhelmed with anticipation. *Why me? Is this good or bad? Will it change my life?*

As you enter the Oval Office, he beckons you to sit with him. He begins by asking you about your life and then tells you about his own. You begin to soften, learning the humanity of the figure in front of you but simultaneously humbled to be in a room of such history and power. As the meeting progresses, he gets down to why you are there.

"I brought you here," he begins "to tell you a few things. I have some commitments I'd like to make to you. First, you have gotten our attention, and we see great promise in your life. So I'd like to commit to you today that whatever you need to accomplish your goals, I've got it covered. Finances, mentors, housing—all you have to do is ask, and I'll give it. I also want to tell you that you can do it at your own pace. The opportunity will never go away or be taken away."

Before you met the president, you studied him and understood something about his nature, but now you've learned how he relates to you as an individual—and everything you've learned comes in the form of commitments and promises to you. How would you feel? I'm guessing you would leave that meeting with a spring in your step, at the very least. You'd still have a lot of work to do to achieve your dreams, but you'd also know that someone powerful believes in you and has your back. You'd realize that life would be completely different from this point on.

When you pursue your dreams, it is vitally important to know not only the nature and attributes of God but also the nature of God toward *you*. To learn more about this aspect of God's nature, we're going to explore three of his promises—the kind of promises that will put a spring in your step because you know that the Dream Giver has your back. These are his commitments to you, and you can rely on his promises.

You Are Pursued

Christ proved God's passionate love for us by dying in our place while we were still lost and ungodly! (Romans 5:8 TPT)

Where could I go from your Spirit?
Where could I run and hide from your face?
If I go up to heaven, you're there!
If I go down to the realm of the dead, you're there too!
If I fly with wings into the shining dawn, you're there!
If I fly into the radiant sunset, you're there waiting!
Wherever I go, your hand will guide me;
your strength will empower me.
It's impossible to disappear from you
or to ask the darkness to hide me,
for your presence is everywhere, bringing light into
     my night. (Psalm 139:7–11 TPT)

God is always with us. His presence can be felt everywhere. This is amazing. But Jesus takes this idea up a notch. The story of the prodigal son is the story of a father who is waiting with bated breath for the son to return. It's the story of a father who runs to his son. It's the story that tells us that God is in pursuit of us more than we are in pursuit of him.

Let's go to that story.

It's been a long time since the son left home, but his father is still watching and waiting. He's still straining his eyes to the horizon, looking for a shimmer of hope that the son might return. Waiting. Wanting. Hoping. Knowing the depth of his son's reckless and depraved foolishness and yet yearning after him.

Then it happens. The moment the father sees his son, the fireworks of love go off. The father does everything he probably shouldn't. He throws all the parenting books out the window. He casts aside his anger and lectures. What follows is one of the most beautiful and moving moments in all of Scripture.

> "From a long distance away, his father saw him coming, *dressed as a beggar*, and great compassion swelled up in his heart for his son who was returning home. So the father raced out to meet him. He swept him up in his arms, hugged him dearly, and kissed him over and over with tender love." (Luke 15:20 TPT)

It's the story of the prodigal son—and it's your story and mine.

You were and are pursued by God. It may be one of the most counterintuitive truths from the Bible. It's the thing that separates Christianity from all other religions—instead of human beings chasing after God, God chases after human beings. Driven by love, God runs toward the child who rejected him, the child who violated every principle and squandered every privilege. And God embraces that child with abandon. It is a beautiful picture of God that is unique to followers of Jesus.

Jesus doesn't wait for you to clean up your act before he invites you in. While you were yet sinful and messed up, Jesus gave it all for you. He knows all about you. He knows about last night. He knows about that night fifteen years ago. And he still loves, pursues, and woos you. It's the beauty of this gospel that has fueled generations of dreamers and missionaries and church planters to give their all back to Jesus.

Pursuing God is noble, but God's pursuit of human beings—his pursuit of you and me—is a whole other kind of beautiful recklessness. And God pursues not only a wayward child in a two-thousand-year-old parable, he pursues you too.

This is a beautiful promise for the dreamer. He's planning the seasons in our lives that direct our paths. He's setting the table before we show up for the meal. He's charting the course before we set sail. I know, *Ryan, stick with one metaphor!*

As you step out, you begin to realize that God has been planning and leading your dream far before you even had it. No trial or disappointment shocks him. No insurmountable odds deter him. No fork in the road confuses him, because he was there *before* you. And as you move toward your dream, the more you will see God running to meet you on the road he has already been on. It's the path he laid out before you took your first breath, the path from which he lovingly beckons you. This is the greatest promise a dreamer can hold on to: the God that calls you planned and pursued that calling before the foundations of the earth. You are in good hands.

You Will Be Equipped

Brothers and sisters, think of what you were when you were called. Not many of you were wise by human standards; not many were influential; not many were of noble birth. But God chose the foolish things of the world to shame the wise; God chose the weak things of the world to shame the strong. God chose the lowly things of this world and the despised things—and the things that are not—to nullify the things that are, so that no one may boast before him. (1 Corinthians 1:26–29)

I am sure of this, that he who began a good work in you will bring it to completion at the day of Jesus Christ. (Philippians 1:6 ESV)

These verses are powerful commitments to all dreamers. God did not choose you because you already had all the skills needed to waltz into his calling on your life. You were not chosen because of your great wisdom or talent. He chose to give you a calling, and he will equip you as you walk in it. Our human standards don't apply when God does the choosing.

Nearly every dreamer we read about in the Bible experienced this. David with Goliath. Gideon with the Midianites. Moses with Pharaoh. These were dreamers who had no qualifications to do what God chose them to do. No pedigree, no charisma, no hefty bank account. They were the misfits of God, chosen for greatness before they had the skills, experience, or qualifications to do what they eventually did—kill Goliath, route the Midianites, and free God's people from Pharaoh. They were equipped and trained *after* they were called, and after they started walking in their calling.

If you are waiting for God to fully equip you and remove every risk before you say yes to his call, you will be waiting indefinitely. God's promise to you is this: the minute you say yes and take your first step, he will equip you for that step. Then as you take the next step, he will equip you for that step. Every step toward your dream is an act of faith. Every step requires you to conquer fear. And every step brings more glory to God. How? When you accomplish tasks for which you have no qualifications, it's a sign to the people around you that you have experienced the miraculous equipping of a faithful God.

Your Calling Is Irrevocable

> The gifts and the calling of God are irrevocable. (Romans 11:29 ESV)

Your gifts and calling are irrevocable. You didn't earn them in the first place, and they remain no matter what. When God makes a commitment, he stands by it. Just as he stood by his commitment to the people of Israel even when they wandered, God stands by his commitment to you even when you wander.

Does this promise sound too good to be true? Can you stray and mess up and still have a calling waiting for you? Can God still use you after transgression or brokenness? The answer is yes. An *irrevocable* yes.

The calling of God is irrevocable because it is the fruit of his nature. God is not like human beings. He doesn't second-guess himself or waver in his commitments. If he gives you gifts and a calling, he won't take them away. If he plants a vision and a dream in your heart, he does so on purpose.

God chose you. He gifted you. He called you. Period. Maybe you have walked away from using your gifts. Maybe you've made some big mistakes and think you've forfeited your calling. You haven't. It's right where you left it. It may be a hard and painful journey, but you can go back. And when you do, God's irrevocable gifts and calling will be there waiting for you.

✦ ✧

The three attributes and the three promises of God we studied just barely scratch the surface. I hope they motivate you to learn even more about who God is and what he is like. The deeper you dive into his nature, the more equipped you'll be to perceive your own calling. The clearer your understanding of the rock-solid nature of the Dream Giver, the more faith you'll have as you become a dream pursuer. This faith is a big part of the foundation that enables you to explode out of your shell and to begin pursuing your dream—or to begin pursuing it again. These are the revelations that will fill you with faith and confidence as you step out.

Understanding God's character is also the foundation that prepares you for the rough seas ahead. Knowing the nature of the Dream Giver is the dream pursuer's secret weapon for fighting off the dream killers.

And make no mistake, there are dream killers out there.

PART 2
THE DREAM KILLERS

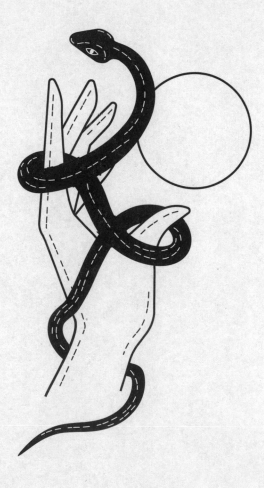

CHAPTER 5

THE CRITIC

When you step out and start to pursue your dream, the critics will inevitably emerge to scoff at you and dissuade you. Critics enjoy pointing out your faults and inabilities. Critics are quick to list all the reasons your dream won't work. Critics would love to see you give up in the face of the "real world." Remember Curmudgeon? He gave up on his dreams, so he resents anyone who hasn't given up on theirs. That's the critic.

And critics are everywhere—school, work, home—every-where.

But as pervasive as critics are, they break down into two camps. First, we have the *external* critic—anyone who hurls judgment from the outside. This can be friends, family, coworkers, social media lookie loos—anyone who isn't *you*. The second camp is the *internal* critic. These are the unhealthy identities we carry, the voices in our head that remind us of our failures or inabilities, our internal monologue of fear or judgment.

The more you step out and move toward your dream, the more you should expect to encounter *both* critics. They carry different challenges and different antidotes, but both will inevitably rear their ugly heads.

THE EXTERNAL CRITIC

Let's start with the external critic. The external critic is the person (or people) who tell you what they don't like about you or your work. Maybe they think you could do something better or have some suggestions on how to improve. Or maybe they are there to tell you your hair looks stupid and that the work you do sucks. No matter what their critique or motivation, the external critic is there to tell you what they don't like. And sometimes what they don't like is just . . . you. External critics have been around a long time and won't stop showing up anytime soon. Let's look at a dastardly critic who reared his ugly head all the way back in the fifth century BC.

Nehemiah and Sanballat

Sanballat the Horonite was a grown-up version of the schoolhouse bully. He was a dastardly critic who sought to end the dreams of a man named Nehemiah. I'm not sure why, but I always picture Sanballat as one of those vaudeville villains hiding in the shadows, twisting the ends of his pointy mustache, holding his cape up to his eyeballs, waiting to catch Nehemiah in a fail so he can knock him down a peg or two. And as any great villain, Sanballat had two doofy sidekicks, Geshem and Tobiah. I picture these guys as pudgy stooges—Crabbe and Goyle to Sanballat's Draco—always mindlessly agreeing with their leader while standing behind him with fists clenched. I think I'm off topic . . .

Nehemiah was the cupbearer to Artaxerxes, king of Persia. Nehemiah was a captive to those who were high up. He was a servant to the politically powerful. But the thing about Nehemiah that I want us to hone in on is that he was a man with a dream. He dreamed of leaving the palace he was enslaved to and returning to repair his homeland, a homeland that was in a state of disrepair. He yearned so much for this dream that he made a plan. He understood the difficulties ahead, but he was mentally ready. He was prepared. Nehemiah didn't only have a dream, he pursued it with his readiness. He was faithfully waiting for that miraculous day when the people of power would inexplicably turn to him and ask him about his dream.

His opportunity arrives in Nehemiah chapter 2.

> The king then asked me, "So what do you want?"
>
> Praying under my breath to the God-of-Heaven, I said, "If it please the king, and if the king thinks well of me, send me to Judah, to the city where my family is buried, so that I can rebuild it."
>
> The king, with the queen sitting alongside him, said, "How long will your work take and when would you expect to return?"
>
> I gave him a time, and the king gave his approval to send me.
>
> Then I said, "If it please the king, provide me with letters to the governors across the Euphrates that authorize my travel through to Judah; and also an order to Asaph, keeper of the king's forest, to supply me with timber for the beams of The Temple fortress, the wall of the city, and the house where I'll be living." (Nehemiah 2:4–8 MSG)

Nehemiah had a dream, a God-given dream to rebuild Jerusalem, the city where his family was from. Us dreamers should take note: he knew exactly what he needed to make his dream a reality. He had his elevator pitch memorized. He knew not only what he needed but also how long it would take.

This had to be one of the most exciting moments of Nehemiah's life. I picture him leaving the room of the king smiling and saying, "I can't believe that just happened!" It's the joy and euphoria that dreamers feel when their dream starts to take off.

When Nehemiah arrives in Jerusalem with his team, they decide that the wall around the city is the first thing that needs repairing. So they jump in and get to work. Nehemiah's vision is about to be realized! What could possibly go wrong?

Enter Sanballat. He's lurking in the shadows, twisting his mustache, and plotting his verbal assault. Critic that he is, he wants to inflict maximum damage, and so he times his entry for just the right moment—the launch of the dream.

> When Sanballat the Horonite, Tobiah the Ammonite official, and Geshem the Arab heard about it, they laughed at us, mocking, "Ha! What do you think you're doing? Do you think you can cross the king?"
>
> I shot back, "The God-of-Heaven will make sure we succeed. We're his servants and we're going to work, rebuilding. You can keep your nose out of it. You get no say in this—Jerusalem's none of your business!" (Nehemiah 2:19–20 MSG)

Ha! What do you think you're doing? Sounds like a critic to me. Now, as we get into the mind of the critic, I want to say this: some critics want to see you get better, and some critics are simply intent on your downfall. Sanballat is the latter. He isn't giving Nehemiah feedback so he can get better; this critic enjoys the smackdown and gets satisfaction from the prospect of Nehemiah's failure.

I don't know Sanballat's backstory, but I think most critics likely had a dream once. A dream that woke them up in the middle of the night. A dream that created a childlike wonder in their heart. A dream they most likely started to pursue. Then a critic hit them. They experienced the harsh, graceless assault of the world and chose to harden their hearts as a form of self-protection. In the face of adversity, they gave up on their dream and became callous.

Then in walks another dreamer—you. And the self-protective alarms go off because you remind them of the dream they gave up on, the dream that caused them pain and immense disappointment. So critics instinctively want to stop other dreamers. They may even convince themselves that they are looking out for your well-being, but deep down they feel threatened because your dream only reminds them of what they gave up. Keep your critic's backstory in mind. Have compassion on them. Your critic was once a dreamer like you, and if you aren't careful, you might one day become a critic yourself.

As a dreamer, you must anticipate this kind of critic. You have to examine their critique and see whether any of it is geared to benefit you, which we will dive deeper into later. But sometimes there is nothing valuable in the critique. Notice what Sanballat says: "Ha! What do you think you're doing? Do you think you can cross the king?" This is not a critique that is meant to help Nehemiah; it's meant to discourage and sideline him. When you hear a critique, try to separate yourself from your emotions and *think* about the words flying at you. If they don't point out any areas of improvement, do your best to put them behind you and respond as Nehemiah did: "God will see me through this! This is *his* calling on me, and I have work to do. Get out of my way!"

Let's be honest. This sort of dismissal is easier when it comes from acquaintances or is hurled at you on social media. But what about the people close to you? What happens when you can't simply dismiss the critic, because they are a friend or family?

I was sharing my dream—the dream that would eventually become OUTCRY—with everyone I could. In my mind it was *going* to happen. It might take another ten years of work, and it might not look exactly as I thought, but my passion for the idea was white hot.

I talked to anyone who would listen about how we needed more unity among the influencers in the worship world and how this could influence the church to be more unified. I talked about how big worship events could be discouraging to local church folks and that, if we weren't careful, people might leave these events more focused on their church's shortcomings than its importance. I cast a vision for events that would encourage local churches and speak life to them.

My dream was grand. Audacious. Bigger than life. And it rubbed people the wrong way—especially when they knew where I came from. Why? Because I came from the same place they did. *Aren't big dreams like that for people who are different from us? People with doctorates and a lot more life experience?*

Out of every corner crept the critics.

Now, critics I didn't know, or barely knew, never bothered me much. But when the critics were those close to me? That hurt.

One day I was sitting in a meeting room full of people who knew me well when one of my friends unexpectedly turned to me and said, "Ryan, why don't you tell us what you and I were talking about last week? You know, that OUTCRY thing." Suddenly, everyone's eyes were on me. I probably turned red. I often turn red when I get sudden attention. I get it from my mom. Thanks, Mom.

So I dove in. I recounted every detail of my audacious dream: Psalm 133, unity of the influencers, the power of the local church, events that would encourage and empower the local while displaying the unity of the global. This was my dream. I could have recited it in my sleep. Then I wrapped up, confident I had sold everyone in the room on the rock-solid and inevitable nature of my dream.

Blank stares. Crickets. Awkward shifting in seats.

Finally, one of them, the wise sage of the group, spoke up. This was the person I looked up to most and who had the greatest influence over me. I expected a resounding, faith-boosting pat on the back, an exclamation of his pride that I carried the vision for such a grand dream. But no.

He began by ticking off an extensive list of why this dream would never happen. He noted the insurmountable obstacles in front of me and proclaimed the naivete of such endeavors. He wrapped up by saying, "You know what you should do instead . . ." and rattled off a list of ideas that were a lot more "realistic." Things that I knew were *easier* but that I also knew deep down were different from what God was saying.

I walked out of that meeting deflated and overcome by a flood of thoughts and emotions that were difficult to detangle. *Wasn't he supposed to encourage me? What am I doing in a place that doesn't support my dreams? Maybe he's right. Should I really be pursuing this crazy dream?*

To be fair, he wasn't wrong. All his points were technically correct and based on many years of experience. He was trying to look out for me by giving me a heads up about the harsh realities I would face. And later I did face many of them.

But what he didn't understand, and therefore couldn't acknowledge, was that God was behind my dream. It was something only God and I were in on. My closest friends weren't in on it. My family wasn't in on it. This was a dream between God and me. It was God's commissioning I needed to hold on to. It was his words and his anointing I needed in order to move ahead. And that's a lesson I could learn only through the pain of rejection from someone I looked up to. I only truly relied on the approval of God over the approval of human beings when I realized that the people around me were fallible. God's approval does not guarantee the approval of other human beings. It never has. It never will.

Believe it or not, what started as *destructive* criticism became *constructive* criticism. Not because the information changed but because my filter changed. I realized—after some prayerful filtering—that unlike Sanballat, my critic was not trying to *derail* me but to *prepare* me with his wisdom and experience.

I'm thankful that he is someone who is still in my life. Today I consider him one of my biggest champions and encouragers. Had I abandoned that relationship, I would have missed out on the wisdom and support he continues to provide.

Okay. Let's shift gears back to our poster-child dreamer—Joseph. Remember that his critics were his family. He couldn't simply throw out their words as Nehemiah did with Sanballat. And for Joseph, the moment came when the tables turned, and how he handled that can teach us a lot about a proper heart-posture toward our critics.

Joseph and His Brothers

Back in chapter 2, we talked about Joseph and his big dreams —the kind of dreams that made his brothers want to kill him. Fast forward through years of slavery, false accusations, and prison, and God's dream for Joseph is finally about to be realized.

After thirteen years of struggle and pain, Joseph is in the exact place God promised he would be—and that's when his old critics show up. His brothers—the ones who didn't believe his calling, rebuked him, and, oh, by the way, sold him into slavery— now come to him for help. But shockingly, Joseph doesn't stick it to them. Instead, he responds with grace and gives them all a safe place to live in Pharaoh's kingdom.

Then Joseph's father dies, and his brothers are understandably a bit nervous. They aren't sure whether Joseph's grace will continue now that Dad is gone.

> When Joseph's brothers saw that their father was dead, they said, "It may be that Joseph will hate us and pay us back for all the evil that we did to him." So they sent a message to Joseph, saying, "Your father gave this command before he died: 'Say to Joseph, "Please forgive the transgression of your brothers and their sin, because they did evil to you."' And now, please forgive the transgression of the

servants of the God of your father." Joseph wept when they spoke to him. His brothers also came and fell down before him and said, "Behold, we are your servants." But Joseph said to them, "Do not fear, for am I in the place of God? *As for you, you meant evil against me, but God meant it for good, to bring it about that many people should be kept alive, as they are today.* So do not fear; I will provide for you and your little ones." Thus he comforted them and spoke kindly to them. (Genesis 50:15–21 ESV, emphasis added)

Remember, Joseph's brothers were the critics who wanted to see him fail. They were the critics who never believed he would be in this place of influence. But the thing these critics meant for evil, God meant for good. Joseph had compassion on the critics in his life because he knew that his brothers didn't understand his calling. They didn't understand that it was God who had placed the audacious dream in Joseph's heart.

You may have critics bearing down on you right now. Maybe they are close to you. Maybe it hurts. A lot. But here's the thing. If God has placed a dream and a calling in your heart, then he will fulfill it. What you need to hold on to most, in the midst of critique, is a word from God. You need to hear what he says about you. That's why a big part of your foundation as a dreamer is a proper understanding of your identity. That's what enables you to rest in the calling Jesus has for you—and allows you to consider the possibility that a critic's presence may be there to make you better. They may be there to alert you to future roadblocks on your journey. They may be there because they have good insight and experience that you should listen to. They may simply be there as a thorn in your side to make you tougher.

It's really something only God and time can make clearer for you. But remember, despite poor packaging and careless words, that critic is placed in your path for a reason.

Trust in this: your harshest critics may be the very ones that launch you into the destiny God has for you.

✧ ✧

I have a degree in fine arts from the University of Arizona. I studied artists and art history. I studied graphic design, photography, and typography. School filled my head with color theory and architectural philosophy. I learned about the zealous nature of the Bauhaus style and how many versions of the same painting Van Gogh would paint—which seems the most probable reason for cutting off his own ear. But of all the valuable lessons I learned in art school, one lesson stands out above all the others. It was the thing most of us art students dreaded in the beginning but eventually learned to love in a hurts-so-good sort of way.

It was a lesson called *critique*.

Now, if you haven't been to art school, let me paint the picture for you (pun intended). Being a student in an art class isn't just free time as it was in kindergarten finger painting. We had purposeful and specific projects to complete, such as creating an image that represented something personal, provided some sort of social commentary, or used a specific style or technique. And once an assignment was complete, we didn't hand it in only to be graded and returned in private. *Nooo.* The teachers inevitably had us put our pieces of art up at the front of the room so everyone could critique them. Some comments were polite and encouraging. Some were benign and pointless. And others were brutal. And many times the most brutal comments came from the teacher.

I had a photography class with one such teacher. Let's call her Agatha. Agatha was tough and had no problem telling you that your photo was lame. Or that your execution was terrible. Or that your photo was meaningless. Every student dreaded critique day in Agatha's class. But what we dreaded most was the critique that came on the last day of class.

Agatha was not the kind of teacher who threw a party or took it easy on you at the end. No. Agatha had us all line up outside her office and then called us in one at a time so she could tell us what she thought about our work that semester. And she held nothing back. Those of us waiting in line often saw students leave her office in tears. Then with hearts beating wildly, we each took a reluctant step forward—one step closer to her office and our impending doom.

When it was my turn, I entered Agatha's office and sat down, but she remained standing, a slight smile on her face. Imagine a lion standing over a wounded gazelle, or Miss Trunchbull before she threw students into the "Chokey." Then Agatha laid into me. She started by pointing out the faults in my work—the faults I was most self-conscious about. She hit every soft spot she could find and noted every little point where my work fell short. She had detailed notes on every artistic commandment she'd seen me break. To Agatha, critique was an art form, and she was a master.

I'm not sure why, but I kept taking classes from her. And as the semesters went by, Agatha's list of my artistic faults grew shorter. Her disapproval of my work slowly shifted to respect. Not only was my work getting better, but my ability to handle critique was improving as well. I no longer felt defensive and offended. Instead, I took her feedback in a professional and measured fashion. I took it as an opportunity to make my work better. We all did.

Using critique to improve my skills was the most valuable lesson I took away from art school. It changed my life. At some point along the way, my fear of critique turned into a hunger for it. I loved how it helped me to grow and improve. But for this to happen, I had to develop a healthy separation between me and my work. I had to get to the point where I understood that *who* I am is not *what* I do.

This principle is not only for the artist, it's a principle for all of us. Don't confuse *what* you do with *who* you are. If you are a teacher or a parent or a business executive, the principle is the same. You are not your role or your job or whatever it is you spend most of your days doing. Remember, your identity is found in your Creator, not in what you create. So to create something beautiful—to realize your dream—you have to develop a healthy separation between who you are and what you do.

One of the best ways I know to do that is to open yourself up to critique. Ask people around you for feedback about your project. Ask people close to you for feedback about how to improve your parenting or your business plan. Ask the questions that scare you. Ask the questions that may have painful answers.

You may be wondering, *Why? Why would I seek out painful feedback? Is it only to get better at my work?* Embracing constructive feedback will definitely help your work, but that's not the most important reason to seek out critique. No. The most important reason to seek out critique is to destroy the stronghold of fear in your life and to prepare yourself for even bigger battles to come. If you live in fear of what others think, you will put your energy into creating a wall of self-protection rather than building a road to your dreams. The problem with walls is that they don't move—which means you'll be stuck hiding behind them. That makes it hard to run after your dreams.

If you want to keep moving into your dreams and calling, you have to face your fears head-on. You have to come to grips with the fact that your work may represent you, but it isn't *you*. And when you have a healthy barrier between *what you do* and *who you are*, you will be able to keep running forward. You will run toward your dreams unhindered by the debilitating fear of other people's opinions.

THE INTERNAL CRITIC

As difficult as it is to overcome the dastardly external critic, every dreamer has to face an even more potent force. This force is the internalization of the external critic. The internal critic is loud. The internal critic is that tape playing over and over in the dreamer's mind. The tape of every weakness. Every lie or false identity ever heard by the dreamer. And the internal critic is a potent foe. I've been battling mine for almost as long as I can remember.

I was the firstborn of three kids in my family, but my brother, Tom, didn't show up till I was seven, and I was fourteen when my sister, Lisa, came along—I guess my parents felt a special connection to the number seven. So I spent the first big chunk of my childhood hanging out with my parents in a quiet house and having adult-level discussions, often until late into the evening.

Mom was a teacher, and Dad was a mechanic putting himself

through engineering school at the University of Arizona. So our little family came from hard work and thoughtful conversation. Dad and I would often lie on our backs in the backyard, look up at the night sky, and talk about black holes or the space-time continuum. We discussed how gravity affected time or how fast light traveled. When my boisterous and energetic uncle Joe sometimes came to visit, he often laughed at our easygoing ways and called us the "quiet family." We *were* quiet—and I liked it. I started life in a thoughtful, quiet little bubble that was comforting and peaceful to me.

And then I had to go to school.

The worst moment of my day was when my mom or dad dropped me off in the morning. I opened the passenger door of our little Toyota Camry and was immediately blasted with an explosion of sound from kids playing on the playground and teachers blowing their whistles. It felt like an unbearable assault. Then, as if that weren't bad enough, I had to go find my friends and start playing. I didn't want to start playing, but I had to— nobody wants to be that weird kid sitting alone in the corner. So I forced my feet to start walking, and I used a lot of self-talk. *No matter how bad you want to go back home, you can't. Don't be the weirdo kid in the corner. Things will get easier if you just get started. And, hey, pretty soon the bell will ring, and you can go inside and sit quietly at your desk.*

But once I was in class, I had to battle another fear: being called on. If the teacher asked me to read something out loud or to answer a question, my face turned red—*thanks again, Mom*—and I stumbled all over my words. It was annoying. It was embarrassing. And it's a feeling I still get whenever I have to speak in front of people. My face goes flush, my heart beats fast, and a voice inside my head starts in with the lies. Cue the internal critic. *You aren't any good at speaking. You stutter and lock up when you speak. You've been like this since childhood. Don't you know that you shouldn't speak in front of other people? Don't you know that you are no good at using your voice? Why haven't you given up on that yet?*

The internal critic can be brutal. It's the voice that hits you in soft places. It reminds you of your inability to keep relationships or tell you that you aren't a great businessperson. It tells you that you're not attractive enough or a strong enough leader. It hits you in your identity and reminds you of all that makes you ashamed. The internal critic is much more dangerous than the external.

Stories such as those of Nehemiah and Joseph can teach us how to deal with external critics, but the Bible also gives us a lot of insight when it comes to the internal critic as well. We need to see the consequences of listening to the internal critic from God's perspective. For that we need to look at one of the most iconic figures in history.

You Can Say No

Here's the thing about God's calling: you can say no.

I think many people believe that God's calling comes to fruition only if you feel ready to do it. That it's reserved for you until you want it. The inner critic can cause you to be so frozen by fear and insecurity that you forfeit something God wants for you. When you say no or not now, God may call on someone else—like a pinch hitter in baseball—who can step in to take your turn at bat.

Remember, your calling is irrevocable—God never yanks it. But you are always free to decline it. God's calling requires your free will. God will not violate your freedom by forcing you to walk in your calling, which means that even though your calling isn't revocable, it is forfeitable. God is sovereign, but you always have a choice. God doesn't force humans into conformity with his will. He allows us to choose, even when the choice grieves him.

Let's focus on Moses's story. We'll pick up the story after he has already encountered the burning bush, watched God turn his staff into a snake and back again, and had his hand made instantly leprous and then whole again. In other words, Moses has seen tangible proof of God's presence and power. But even miracles were not enough to drown out the voice of his internal critic.

> But Moses said to the LORD, "Oh, my Lord, I am not eloquent, either in the past or since you have spoken to your servant, but I am slow of speech and of tongue." (Exodus 4:10 ESV)

Moses has witnessed God's power on the external world, but it hasn't yet translated into faith that God has power on his internal world. Maybe Moses flashed back to that Egyptian schoolhouse he attended. Maybe he remembered how the other kids made fun of his inability to speak well when the teacher had him read his social studies papyrus out loud. Wherever that idea of his inadequacies came from, Moses latched on to it and never let it go.

By this point in his life, he has given a loud voice to his internal critic by laying out his insecurities. Here's how God responds:

> The LORD said to him, "Who gave human beings their mouths? Who makes them deaf or mute? Who gives them sight or makes them blind? Is it not I, the LORD? Now go; I will help you speak and will teach you what to say."

But Moses said, "Pardon your servant, Lord. Please send someone else."

Then the LORD's anger burned against Moses and he said, "What about your brother, Aaron the Levite? I know he can speak well. He is already on his way to meet you, and he will be glad to see you. You shall speak to him and put words in his mouth; I will help both of you speak and will teach you what to do. He will speak to the people for you, and it will be as if he were your mouth and as if you were God to him." (Exodus 4:11–16)

So Moses persists in his insecurity. His commitment to the internal critic outweighs his trust in God's calling. His need to hold on to the idea that he's no good at speaking trumps his faith that God can overcome his inabilities. And no words or even miraculous signs from God can convince him otherwise. And God knows it. It grieves him, but he recognizes that Moses has made his choice.

In steps Aaron, the pinch hitter. Batter up.

God has a calling for you. It's beautiful and beyond what you think you are capable of. God sees potential in you that you can't see in yourself, and he looks right at you and says, "I want you." Then it's up to you to say yes. It's up to you to begin walking. You are completely free to choose. You can wave your hands in protest and say, "Oh, no, God. You don't want me. I'm no good at that. Please pick someone else."

God will speak to you. He will show you he is trustworthy and able to overcome your fears. He will seek to show you he has power to overcome any and all of your shortcomings. But in the end, if you say no, he has a pinch hitter. He will not force you into your calling.

Moses, you're up! What, you're saying no? Are you sure? Okay. Aaron, you're up! Your answer is yes? Good. Let's go!

It hits me in the gut when I read "the LORD's anger burned against Moses" when Moses's insecurities led him to say no to God. At first it bothered me. Don't we have a good Father? How can a good Father get mad at his child when his child is afraid and insecure? But then I started thinking about it from God's perspective.

I am a father, and I love my kids immensely, but I do get angry with them. All fathers do at times. I can get angry when they don't listen or when they hurt each other. I get angry when they treat other people with disrespect or bring a running hose into the house. Anyway, you get the point—there are lots of ways children can make a parent legit angry.

All these challenges are the routine stuff of parenting, but one thing makes me especially angry. It's watching my children surrender in a self-imposed battle. It makes me angry when they believe something about themselves that isn't true. It makes me angry when they allow a mean comment from a kid at school to seep into their internal monologue. It makes me angry when they choose to believe something about their character or abilities that is untrue. It makes me wish I could do something—make that decision for them or change that thought pattern—so they can see the potential that I see in them.

But I can't. I can't have self-esteem for my kids. I can't make them see themselves the way I see them. The best I can do is to tell them and show them and pray that it sinks in.

God tried to tell Moses about his calling and tried to show Moses his power, and Moses still said no. This frustrated God. It angered him that one of his children would choose shame, insecurity, and the inner critic over the power, freedom, and loving affirmations of a Father.

God's response to Moses reminds me of another situation in which two people decided to listen to a voice other than God's. It happened way back in Genesis. On the advice of the serpent, Adam and Eve ate forbidden fruit, discovered they were naked, covered themselves with fig leaves, and hid from God. Then God asked a sizzling and painful question, "Who told you that you were naked?" (Genesis 3:11). Adam and Eve believed a lie—and then they ate it. They internalized a lie that caused spiritual death and decay. They allowed the internal critic to move in and take up residence.

We do the same thing when we allow the voices of our internal critics to fill us with shame for our past mistakes, our inabilities, our insecurities. Then we hide when the voice of God calls to us, Who told you that you were ugly? Who told you that you are no good at what I've called you to do? Who told you that I won't be with you? Who told you that you're a bad leader or an awkward person or that you don't have what it takes? Who told you (insert your own issues here)?

God isn't asking for information. He already knows the sources of the internal critic's lies. God asks the questions to point out that he is not the one telling you these things. But you are free to choose what voice to listen to—and your choice matters. It could mean the difference between walking into or forfeiting the dream God has for you.

This is why I call the critic a dream killer. There is an enemy out there seeking to sideline you. The voices you choose to listen to can change your destiny. God is committed to you and his will to be done on earth is real, tangible, and includes you. But if you choose to sit on the bench, there will be a pinch hitter God can use in your place.

I believe Moses would have experienced even more blessing and anointing than he did had he trusted God in every aspect of his calling. Did God still use Moses? Yes, of course he did. Can God still use you if you say no to an aspect of your calling? Of course he can. But you'll be pursuing your calling with a limp. You'll be withholding some of yourself from God. You'll always feel as though you could lean in more. And there will likely be bitterness at those pinch hitters who step in for you.

Here's the bottom line. Don't let the critics—external or internal—dictate what you will entrust to God. Don't let the critics rob you of the anointing and calling God has for you. Stand firm on the foundation of God's character and your identity. Stand firm on the truth of what God says about you when nobody else is saying it. Stand firm on what God says about you, even when you don't see it in yourself. Embrace your freedom. Be the dreamer who refuses to listen to voices that don't originate from God. Be the dreamer who is in the habit of saying yes.

You can choose to ignore the voices that speak at you, but the voices that speak in you are much harder to ignore. They burrow deep and take root only to steal your joy. And, as they did with Moses, they can even cause you to forfeit your calling. When you don't understand who God created you to be and you don't fully grasp the nature of the Dream Giver, you will naturally fall back on insecurities—the internal voices that remind you of your weaknesses, the internal voices that try to drown out the voice of your Creator.

So what are your internal voices saying? What weakness or hurt or insecurity do they repeatedly remind you of? What hurtful comment spoken to you in childhood or young adulthood plays on constant repeat?

Some of these voices may be so familiar that they no longer even have to speak to be heard. When the lies of your critic are fully internalized, they become part of your operating system, and you begin to act on them without thinking. That means you could have reflexive moves of self-protection you may not even be aware of. These need to be sought out in prayer. These are the hardwired lies of the internal critic that need to be identified and silenced by God.

Take some time to pray and ask. It isn't a mystical skill. It's not rocket science. It's creating some quiet space so you can take out a blank sheet of paper and write down what you think God is saying. God desires to speak to his children, so ask with expectancy, and ask more than once. Maybe get together with a friend or a pastor who can listen to God with you. No matter how you approach it, you must identify the lies of your internal critic. They pose some of the greatest threats to your dream. They are cancerous. They have the power to keep you in a state of fear and inaction. They can truly kill your dream. The internal critic can even shift someone else into your calling. Not by God's choice but by yours.

You Can Get Derailed

Let's look at the story of Elijah, a biblical dreamer who is fearless and full of faith, a prophet who challenges the prophets of Baal to a duel of the gods. It's seriously a dramatic story.

Let me set the scene. Elijah is fed up with his people worshiping idols. He wants his people to see the true power of Yahweh over the worthless idols of Baal, so he proposes a high-stakes showdown.

Elijah went before the people and said, "How long will you waver between two opinions? If the LORD is God, follow him; but if Baal is God, follow him."

But the people said nothing.

Then Elijah said to them, "I am the only one of the LORD's prophets left, but Baal has four hundred and fifty prophets. Get two bulls for us. Let Baal's prophets choose one for themselves, and let them cut it into pieces and put it on the wood but not set fire to it. I will prepare the other bull and put it on the wood but not set fire to it. Then you call on the name of your god, and I will call on the name of the LORD. The god who answers by fire—he is God."

Then all the people said, "What you say is good." (1 Kings 18:21–24)

Elijah throws down the challenge. It's a faith-filled, no-margin-for-error public challenge. The prophets of Baal dance around the altar, screaming and cutting themselves, trying to get Baal to show up, but nothing happens. Then Elijah steps up. He has the people pour bucket after bucket of water on the altar, then prays for God to send fire. The result? "Then the fire of the LORD fell and consumed the burnt offering and the wood and the stones and the dust, and licked up the water that was in the trench" (1 Kings 18:38 ESV).

Bam. What a boss! Elijah is one faith-filled maniac of a prophet. He has to be on a spiritual high after that one. And you would think that nothing would derail him after a victory such as this, that nothing could cause him to question his calling or the power of God in his life.

But you would be wrong.

When Queen Jezebel hears of Elijah's dramatic victory over her fellow Baalians, she immediately sends this message to Elijah: "May the gods do to me and more also, if I do not make your life as the life of one of them by this time tomorrow" (1 Kings 19:2 ESV). In other words, prepare to die, because I'm coming for you.

Does our faith-filled maniac of a prophet confidently laugh in her face? I mean, he just saw fire fall from heaven and witnessed the defeat of 450 prophets of Baal. One prophetess challenging him over Twitter can't possibly scare him, right?

But she does. One critic shows up, and he is completely derailed.

> Elijah was afraid and ran for his life. When he came to Beersheba in Judah, he left his servant there, while he himself went a day's journey into the wilderness. He came to a broom bush, sat down under it and prayed that he might die. "I have had enough, Lord," he said. "Take my life; I am no better than my ancestors." (1 Kings 19:3–4)

How melodramatic. Even though he slayed in the smackdown of the gods, a threat from one stinkin' critic sends him running away, and he wants to die. He wallows in self-pity. Elijah couldn't overcome the well-timed challenge of one critic. And that external threat from Jezebel became an internal threat—a cancer—that sunk its tendrils so deeply into his mind that he was unable or unwilling to let it go. The critique sank into Elijah and gained strength. It turned into bitterness. It turned into victimhood. It was an offense that was killing him from the inside out, but he held on to it like a security blanket made of fire. And this self-obsession with his own insecurities effectively took him out of the game. So God appoints a pinch hitter.

God says to Elijah, "Anoint Elisha son of Shaphat from Abel Meholah to succeed you as prophet" (1 Kings 19:16).

This story always amazes me. How does the faith-filled maniac allow fear, self-righteousness, and self-pity to take him out of the lineup? He allows the voice of the external critic to become the voice of the internal critic. He internalizes the toxicity. It becomes part of his operating system and sabotages his calling from the inside out. And nothing even God himself says or does can change his mind.

✧ ✧

"No one knows the thoughts of God except the Spirit of God," wrote the apostle Paul (1 Corinthians 2:11). Ultimately, for us to conquer the critics in our lives, we need to spend time with the one who was given to us as our friend and guide, the Holy Spirit. We need to hear his voice louder than any other voice. When you spend a lot of time listening to the voice of the Holy Spirit, you begin to be able to spot counterfeits easily and more quickly. This shrinks the power of the critics and gives them less of a foothold in your internal dialogue.

The secret of conquering the critics is not succeeding in your dreams so that you can prove them wrong. No, the you truly conquer critics by keeping the external critique from seeping into your internal dialogue and drowning out the voice of God. And when you consistently hear God's voice above the others, the less power you give to the critics. You'll take more risks and be less bothered by failure. Then you'll have the strength to face the next in our list of dream killers out there. This one is subtle, but it has the same power to derail, distract, and even kill your dream.

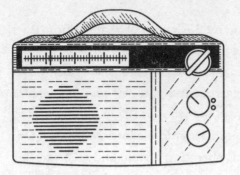

CHAPTER 6

THE NOISE

I'm very driven. When there's opportunity to push an idea through or see a dream take new ground, I rarely hesitate. Nor do I back off. Ever. I'm a shoot-first-ask-questions-later sort of person. And when the circumstances need it, I put my head down and drive forward until I reach my goal.

I think you get it. I push. In some circles it's referred to as *hustle*.

Hustle is a skill that comes in handy when getting a dream off the ground. It's the point in the process when everything is hard. Getting buy-in is hard. Casting vision is hard. Finding resources is hard. And giving up is easy. But this is my playground. These are the problems that get me up in the morning. I look at all the possibilities, pinpoint the best starting point, and pounce.

Hustle is a gift that comes in handy, but it's also a gift that bites back. It can be a curse at times. When I'm chasing a dream, all my being gets wrapped up in it. Every square second—*do seconds come in square units?*—is filled with trying to take advantage of every opportunity. Every day is a day to network. Write. Push. Pounce. And then repeat. It never ends. Hustle never slaps me on the back and says, "Hey, nice work. Take the weekend off!"

The curse of hustle is that it is never satisfied. Nothing is ever done. There is always more to do. And so there have been moments in my life when God had to intervene—to silence the noise of my hustle so he could lead me back to the quiet and still.

◇ ◇

A couple of years ago, I was speaking at an event in Nashville. The event organizers put me up in an amazing hotel. Fancy. Real fancy. As in *too* fancy for a guy born in the dusty western town of Tucson—you know, guns, tumbleweeds, saloons. Believe it or not, I actually did grow up down the street from a saloon. Not important . . . *anyway*. . . .

I arrived the day before I was scheduled to speak, so when I got up the next morning, I had the entire day to myself before I spoke that night. Now, for a dad with young kids, this is an insane luxury. The kind of luxury I didn't want to tell my wife about because she was home with all three of our precious lambs . . . *alone*. So that morning I did what I love to do every morning—I got some coffee, turned on some relaxing music, and read.

It happened to be one of those rare winter days in Nashville when it was cold enough to snow. As I sat in my room and watched the snow falling outside, I felt a quiet peace I hadn't experienced in a long time. That is, until my driven, type-A personality rudely invaded my quiet time. My hustle didn't care that I was happy. It didn't care how peaceful I felt. It wanted me to push and pounce and make things happen.

I began thinking about all the connections I could make. *I'm here all day—and Nashville is filled with people I should meet with, right? I mean, how could I not?* Before I knew it, I was mentally writing plans and proposals for people I didn't know and had yet to contact. In a blink, the hustle had completely taken over.

As I was going over the list of people to call and tasks to push forward, I felt a gentle but clear nudge from God. It was as if a mental stop sign shot up in the middle of my thinking: *Ryan, pause and ask me about it.*

So I paused and asked, "Lord, who should I meet with today?"

The answer was swift. I didn't expect it to be so decisive. It was like a splash of cold water straight to the face.

Me.

Right there in my peaceful, beautiful room, I accepted God's invitation to spend the day with him. And I realized that he had set it all up. The fancy hotel, a room to myself, the peaceful snow outside. He had a plan for that day that did not include hustle. And that day was something I needed more than I realized. Being quiet and still so I could rest in God's presence was more important than anything I could have hustled and "accomplished" that day.

Don't get me wrong. I'm a big believer in hard work. With the apostle Paul, I believe we are "co-workers" with Christ (1 Corinthians 3:9). We work *with* God. This is something we'll unpack more later because I firmly believe we are called to work—yes, even to *hustle*—for the kingdom. And it makes me crazy when I come across people with a, how should I put it, *stunted* kingdom work ethic.

But . . .

There are rhythms in life—some that God commands. We aren't made to work all the time or to rest all the time. We need a healthy rhythm that keeps us from burnout on the one hand and apathy on the other. There is a life-giving, commission-fulfilling nature to being a co-laborer with Christ. Some moments God pushes through our busyness so we can pause and rest. Like the halftime in the Super Bowl or a rest in a musical score, we must routinely surrender to peace amid the noise. Otherwise, the noise will overtake us.

THE GOOD PORTION

When Jesus invited people to follow him, he said:

> "Come to me, all who labor and are heavy laden, and I will give you rest. Take my yoke upon you, and learn from me, for I am gentle and lowly in heart, and you will find rest for your souls. For my yoke is easy, and my burden is light." (Matthew 11:28–30 ESV)

A yoke is a rigid wooden beam that connects two working animals, such as oxen or water buffalo. It helps the animals to keep pace with each other as they pull a plow or a heavy cart. We are connected to Jesus in that way—connected to his pace and his rhythms. We are connected to his broad shoulders, which help us carry the weight of our work. When we are yoked to Christ, he shares the burden, which makes the burden lighter. Yes, we are still working, but we let Jesus set the pace and share the load.

It's a beautiful image that all of us dreamers need to remember. Whenever we try to push too far ahead, we will inevitably take more of the load onto our own shoulders. That makes the yoke hard and the burden heavier. We can try to go faster than Jesus, but then it's only a matter of time before we collapse from fatigue and burnout.

For the driven, workaholic dreamers out there—you know who you are—Jesus's promise of an easy yoke and a light burden is incredibly good news. At times it will challenge you to—dare I say it—stop working and to actually be okay with it. When you take on the easy yoke, you have to let go of that sense of guilt at not "accomplishing" something when you take time out to rest and just be. You have to set aside the hurry and the hustle so you can fall into the rhythm, pace, and burden weight limit set by Jesus. This may be hard for you. It may seem like an unbearable slowness at times, but it will lead to something beautiful and peaceful.

Jesus called it *the good portion.*

✧　✧

The principle of the good portion comes from a familiar story in the Bible—the story of sisters Mary and Martha.

> Jesus entered a village. And a woman named Martha welcomed him into her house. And she had a sister called Mary, who sat at the Lord's feet and listened to his teaching. But Martha was distracted with much serving. And she went up to him and said, "Lord, do you not care that my sister has left me to serve alone? Tell her then to help me." But the Lord answered her, "Martha, Martha, you are anxious and troubled about many things, but one thing is necessary. Mary has chosen the good portion, which will not be taken away from her." (Luke 10:38–42 ESV)

Martha raises a practical concern—there is a long list of work to do, and her sister isn't doing squat to help. But Jesus redirects Martha's attention from a practical concern to a heart concern.

The text says that Martha was "distracted." That begs the question: distracted from what and by what? Answer: she was distracted from Jesus by her "much serving." She allowed her work to take her focus off Jesus. As a result, she became "anxious and troubled about many things."

And then there is Mary, who did not allow herself to be distracted. She sat and listened to Jesus. She chose the good portion. In other words, she chose something better and more important than work. Martha's hustle and distraction robbed her of the good portion.

Martha's problem wasn't that she was working hard. Her problem was that she allowed her work to dominate her instead of subduing and dominating her work. (Remember the Genesis command we talked about in chapter 3?) And it left her distracted, anxious, and troubled, not to mention mad at her sister for not working as hard as she was. Her unhealthy pride in her work caused her to look down on someone she considered a slacker. The condition of her heart at this point is not good. She is overcome with a self-righteous bitterness toward her sister.

Mary has the joy-robbing disease of the workaholic. Having a strong work ethic and healthy pride in your work is good, but only to a point. And if your work leaves you feeling self-righteous bitterness, you're well past that point. You've harnessed yourself to a yoke of your own making, and it is far from easy and light. In fact, it's a cage and you're trapped in it. Now you have become Martha. You resent it when others choose the better portion—to rest and enjoy life.

Workaholic hustle is a disease that can kill your dream. It is as toxic and life-destroying as substance abuse. It claims families and causes heart attacks. It destroys marriages and minds. Even if it initially leads to success, it will catch up with you eventually. One way or another, you'll crash. Maybe it will lead to an affair. Or a mental breakdown. Or a heart attack. It will sneak up on you and rob you of your better portion—and that includes your dream.

Ultimately, this is a disease that stems from an identity rooted in the wrong place. If your identity is found in your hustle—your ability to get ahead and make things happen—you will live in a perpetual never-enough mindset. There will always be "many tasks" to do, many chores to be anxious and troubled about, many things to keep you distracted and overwhelmed.

The good news is that there is a powerful antidote to the diseased never-enough mindset. But be warned if you truly struggle with this, because the cure will likely be painful for you. God takes this condition so seriously that he put his healing prescription in the form of a commandment.

Sabbath.

THE RHYTHM OF SABBATH

Sabbath rest is one of the Ten Commandments for a reason. It even comes before thou shalt not kill, covet, or commit adultery—all things you would think would be at the top of God's list. But the Sabbath comes before all of those. Why? Could it be because tired people are more likely to kill, covet, and commit adultery? Maybe. But there's more to it. Let's read the commandment to see why.

Remember the Sabbath day by keeping it holy. Six days you shall labor and do all your work, but the seventh day is a sabbath to the LORD your God. On it you shall not do any work, neither you, nor your son or daughter, nor your male or female servant, nor your animals, nor any foreigner residing in your towns. For in six days the LORD made the heavens and the earth, the sea, and all that is in them, but he rested on the seventh day. Therefore the LORD blessed the Sabbath day and made it holy. (Exodus 20:8–11)

God himself rested on the seventh day. He had a work-rest rhythm, one he wove into the very fabric of creation. We are created in God's image, which means we are hard-wired to keep the same work-rest rhythm. One day every week, God commands us to truly, deeply, and completely rest. It's in our DNA to need that sort of rest.

God made it a commandment because Sabbath doesn't come naturally—we have to choose it. We have to arrange our lives so that we have at least one day a week in which we do no work. That's the day we allow ourselves to be unproductive. You heard me right, hustle workaholics—*un-pro-duc-tive*. It's a commandment that's simple in principle but often hard in practice. Here's how author and rabbi Abraham Joshua Heschel puts it: "Six days a week we wrestle with the world, wringing profit from the earth; on the Sabbath we especially care for the seed of eternity planted in the soul. The world has our hands, but our soul belongs to Someone Else. Six days a week we seek to dominate the world, on the seventh day we try to dominate the self."[1]

I love that. "The world has our hands, but our soul belongs to Someone Else." For those of us with a wicked case of never-enough-hustleitis, it's easy to wring productivity out of the earth, but it isn't so easy to "care for the seed of eternity planted in the soul." This requires a fundamental shift in perspective. We have to value the health of our soul over the hustle of our to-do list. This is an essential part of a healthy rhythm, and we need to prioritize it and, dare I say, work at it. Ironically, it takes effort to rest. On that seventh day, we dominate our work ethic for the greater good—for the good portion.

When my wife, Blake, and I relocated to Phoenix several years ago, we rented a house, sight unseen. We felt God leading us to Phoenix to take a job with a new church, but the busyness of packing and finishing up my previous job left no time to travel to Phoenix to find a house. When friends told us about a house owned by one of the elders in our new church, we held our breath and signed the lease. Fortunately, the house turned out to be just what we needed.

We loved a lot of things about that house, but it was the raised garden in the backyard that Blake loved most. Now, you have to remember, when you live in the desert, anything green is amazing to you. Water is hard to come by. When it rains, we all stand outside watching it and smiling as though it's a certified miracle. So this backyard garden was a novelty to us. And Blake was determined to wring some green and growing things out of that earth.

It ended up being harder than we thought. First we had to painstakingly remove all the demonic desert weeds, one at a time. We had to get new soil. We had to get seeds and buy gardening equipment. We had to figure out what would grow in 180-degree desert heat. It was a lot of work.

Then we had to tend those seeds, watering them day after day, which is not very satisfying when all you see is bare soil. For weeks we walked to the flower beds every morning with a heavy watering pail, expecting there to be plants but day after day seeing none.

Then one day the plants finally popped out of the soil. Several weeks later they began to produce. It was so satisfying to harvest zucchini and tomatoes and to see sunflowers five feet tall and to smell the other flowers when we walked by. We got a yield of amazing produce by tending to the seeds we had planted. We traded a lot of effort for something greater.

Sabbath rest is a lot like tending a garden. It takes time and effort to remove the weeds and clear the soil. The weeds are the distractions that take your focus off rest. The weeds are "urgent" things that rob you of time and energy. The weeds are anything that hinders you from deep and meaningful recharge. But over time that seed of rest you plant begins to yield the fruit of peace and joy in your life. Daily watering, weekly weeding, seasonal replanting—this is the rhythm of rest in our lives. Watering represents the activities that bring you joy. Replanting symbolizes our seasons of disconnect or relocation. Maybe vacation. Or even sabbatical. Sabbath is not only a one-day-a week kind of rest but rest in many ways and for varying lengths of time as the season requires. The foundational principle of Sabbath is not something we do only weekly. We must also create *daily* moments of Sabbath. And longer, *annual* times of Sabbath. And even *longer* experiences of Sabbath every seven years. Ever heard the word *sabbatical*? All these ideas come from the Bible. The biblical command is to let the land rest from farming every seven years (Leviticus 25:4).

There is no one-size-fits-all when it comes to figuring out the best work-rest rhythm. Rest looks different depending on the person and the season. I heard an old Jewish proverb that goes, "If you work with your mind, Sabbath with your hands. If you work with your hands, Sabbath with your mind." It's basically a change to your day-to-day routine that gives you energy to get back into work recharged.

In this season of your life, what is the most restful, relaxing day you can think of? If you took one day to *treat yo' self*, what would that look like? Be specific. Now, what would a rest-filled two-week vacation look like? If you could have a sabbatical—an extended period of rest—what would that look like? Take a moment to think this through and write it down because rest needs to be on your goal sheet. Your rest path needs to be right there next to your career path when it comes to goals. Plan your rest, and get it on your calendar because if you don't plan it, you won't do it. And remember, the stakes of not doing it are high.

Daily, weekly, and annual rest needs to happen in our lives. And as hard as it is in most careers out there, longer sabbatical rest should happen every seven years. Maybe this happens at a point of career change. Or maybe it's just a long vacation. However you tackle it in your life, these are all extensions of the principle of Sabbath rest, and making them happen requires planning and strategy. Plan and strategize Sabbath the same way you plan and strategize work. Six days a week you dominate at work, on the seventh you dominate yourself to rest and be unproductive.

If you want to see a dream God has given you take off, don't allow lack of Sabbath to steal it from you. Because eventually, it will.

A POVERTY OF ATTENTION

This historic period we're living in has a name. It's called the information age or sometimes the digital age or the new media age. Whatever you call it, it's a period that has experienced the greatest technological shifts in communication since the printing press. We have digital devices that give us instant access to people. We can use a mobile phone to post a picture on social media that instantly travels the world. We have access to endless information at the tips of our fingers. This instant communication and access to information was science fiction not too long ago.

But with all this instant access comes a curse.

Herbert A. Simon was a twentieth-century American economist and social scientist. He made this prophetic statement back in the 1970s that pertains more to today than ever before:

> What information consumes is rather obvious: it consumes the attention of its recipients. Hence a wealth of information creates a poverty of attention and a need to allocate that attention efficiently among the overabundance of information sources that might consume it.[2]

In other words, we have a wealth of information but a poverty of attention. We're constantly distracted. We can't focus. Even more importantly, we can't discern what is worthy of our attention. So we give it to the thing that's right in front of us. Our phones. Email. Social media. It's all at our fingertips. We make a few taps, post or comment, and then we get feedback that our brains consider a reward.

In fact, recent research indicates that the human mind can

readily become addicted to this feedback.[3] When we post on social media and someone responds or likes our post, our brains release a small hit of dopamine—the chemical that we experience as pleasure and positive feedback. The same thing happens when we receive a text message or email from someone. We get a small biochemical reinforcement that what we are doing makes us feel good and should be repeated—a lot. And it's the constant hits of dopamine reinforcing our behavior that can lead to addiction. We're addicted when we're preoccupied with social media or our devices. We're addicted when we constantly check our devices and accounts and feel anxious whenever we don't have access. We're addicted when we neglect relationships and responsibilities in real life to spend more time in our digital worlds. That's as much of an addiction as anything else, my friend.

We don't even have to stick with one digital drug. Why settle for scrolling Instagram when you can scroll Instagram *and* watch Netflix? We can be on multiple devices doing many things simultaneously. Our brains kick into hyperdrive, and we check out from reality. This happens to me all the time.

Let's see what's happening on Instagram. I peruse Instagram for 5.5 seconds before realizing there's nothing new. *Oh, shoot, I forgot to email Kaylee back.* I write a quick email with four typos, and before I even hit send, I realize, *I haven't checked Facebook today.* So I scroll through Facebook for ten minutes before clicking on a Pinterest link on survival (because, you know, *zombies* . . . anyway). And this whole time, I have a Netflix show playing in the background.

Maybe you don't do this. Maybe you have amazing self-discipline and set rules for yourself. Or maybe you live in a cabin you whittled by hand in the middle of the woods and make your own clothes from beaver hides. Good for you. But before you get too judgmental about my habits, you need to know that this is increasingly becoming the norm in our society. It's the curse of rapid technological advancement. And all this multitasking is changing not only the way we think but also the very structure of the brains we think with.

I recently read a study conducted by the University of Sussex that concluded that multitasking with screened devices causes physical alterations to our brains. It reduces the density of our gray brain matter. Authors Kep Kee Loh and Ryota Kanai state, "Media multitasking is becoming more prevalent in our lives today and there is increasing concern about its impacts on our cognition and social-emotional well-being. Our study was the first to reveal links between media multitasking and brain structure."[4]

The distractions of multitasking—hopping quickly back and forth from one thing to the other—keep us from having deep and focused thoughts about any one thing. As we multitask, our brain density literally diminishes. Our ability to give sustained attention to one thing slips away. Over time we find it easier to keep our brains in shallow think mode and therefore dive even deeper into multitasking because it's the only thing capable of occupying our attention.

Okay, so what does this have to do with pursuing a dream and living into your calling? Why are things such as digital addiction and multitasking dream killers? Because when you're routinely preoccupied by a whirlwind of small distractions, days of distraction become weeks of distraction, which then become months of distraction. Months turn into years. Years into decades. That's how the noise of distractions becomes the quiet, slow killer of your dreams.

Distraction doesn't tell you that you can't accomplish your dream; it tells you to do it *later*. It doesn't try to feed you lies; it just tells you that you're too tired right now. It tells you that you should go after your dreams in a less busy season of your life—even though, deep down, you know your seasons have only gotten busier. Distraction overwhelms you with so much background noise that you feel as if you're freaking out even when you're still. It means you never truly rest.

Once again, the antidote to distraction and our poverty of attention is found in the Sabbath.

Tiffany Shlain is a filmmaker and founder of the Webby Awards. She talks a lot about the tension we feel living in the physical world while wrestling with the digital one. She says that she is not religious, but her heritage is Jewish, and she's found that practicing a "digital Shabbat" helps to reset her mind. Here's how she describes her family routine:

> So Friday night we turn off every screen in a very ritualistic way. When we start, we light candles, all the cell phones go off, the TV goes off, and the computers go off. And then we're offline for all of Saturday until after sunset. . . . It's like hitting the reset button on my sense of balance. It has just changed my life profoundly. I tell everyone I know to try it. I feel more present with the people I care about, and also more grounded and more creative. Some people say, "Oh, on vacations, I unplug." But when do vacation happen? Once or twice a year. There's something about the weekly practice of getting a different mode of experiencing the world back that's really important.[5]

This is the insight and wisdom of God that is being "discovered" by secular society. We've talked already about Sabbath, but consider taking a *digital* Sabbath as well.

Our family has started calling our Saturdays "Family Fun Day." We unplug. We go out and explore or ride bikes. Or stay home and read. We reconnect and reset. No social media. No work. Just family fun. And make no mistake, *it's hard*. I have a difficult time unplugging and being, well, unproductive. But it does seem to set my mind at ease. It reduces anxiety and increases my ability to be present with the people I care about.

The distracted dreamer is a sidelined dreamer. Do an audit of your time—nowadays most phones can do that for you. Identify any distractions you could cut out of your day to free up more time for resting, recharging, and dreaming. Turn off the TV. Put your phone away. Spend some uninterrupted time with God. Rest. Do this so you can have not "just-enough" energy but an abundant, rested energy and a renewed space for passion—passion that spills over into your dreaming world. Create space to work on that business plan. Or the album you want to record. Or the book you want to write. You have 168 hours a week at your disposal. Make them count.

CHAPTER 7

THE SETBACK

I was out of town and working in a temporary office. The walls were paper thin, and it was impossible not to hear the tirade between the two strong personalities in the office next to mine. This was the second event I'd done with the guy who was yelling, and it was quickly shaping up to be the last. Then the verbal fireworks suddenly crescendoed. Not good. What I was hearing made me nervous. I turned on some loud music to make sure I wouldn't be overheard and called my wife. "Honey, there's a problem. I need to book a flight so I can come home first thing tomorrow morning."

✧ ✧

The Setback is real. It *will* happen to you. And not just once. It will happen often.

Setbacks are most dangerous to the dreamers who don't expect them. If you expect the road to your dream to move ahead in a predictable straight line, your first setback may be your last. If you are relying on adrenaline and passion to get you through, they won't.

Setbacks can kill your dream because they require you to go through seasons that feel terrible. Those seasons may seem to prove all your critics right. Seasons of failure can cause people to tilt their heads and look at you with pity and ask, "How are you holding up?"

Setbacks suck.

But they also shine a white-hot spotlight on some things you may not be aware of—things you have to deal with if you want to hit a home run with your dream.

STEPPING UP TO BAT

That moment in the office with the tirade going on next door was the second time I'd taken a swing at getting my dream off the ground. And let's just say, my first at bat hadn't gone any better.

First Swing

I had my first setback was when I was nineteen. I was young, optimistic, and ready to tackle my dream. At the time, I played drums in a worship band, and we traveled around Arizona leading worship at churches. But after playing many events for other people, we started talking about doing an event of our own. After a lot of late-night planning-dreaming sessions, we put down a deposit—more money than any of us had ever seen—on an outdoor venue downtown. Our leader and his young wife took on all the financial risk. Our dream was to do an all-day worship event centered on bringing churches together and seeing them impact poverty in the city. We were beyond excited.

Then we got to work.

We spent months driving around to nearly every church in town asking whether they would partner with us. We handed out flyers and spoke to their youth groups, and at the end of months of hard work, many churches said they were with us. We were working hard and feeling good. We planned to bring out one of our favorite worship leaders, Charlie Hall. We even lined up sponsors and figured out food and concessions.

It was all coming together.

At the same time, we were rehearsing together three to four times a week. We had a lot of original songs and began working on a rough album. We had absolutely no idea what we were doing, but that didn't seem to bother any of us. We moved ahead with the kind of naive exuberance only a group of nineteen-year-olds can.

The night before the event, we learned that some people had found out about our event and were not exactly supportive. We found a ton of nasty graffiti on the stage background and even found strange leftovers from a witch's curse ceremony. Yep. Like *real* witches. I know. Tucson is weird. But we did our best to deal with it and kept moving. After cleaning up the graffiti late into the night—and praying off all the curses and bad juju—the big day finally came.

We were there before the sun came up and worked frantically to get it all ready. But as we got close to the start time, we noticed something troubling—and no, it had nothing to do with witches.

When we looked outside, we saw that nobody was lined up. *Nobody.*

We were expecting more than five hundred people at this event. We had flown out one of our worship heroes to perform. We told all our friends and family how big it was going to be.

And suddenly we felt self-conscious. We had nowhere to hide our failed expectations.

All together, there were maybe 150 people that showed up throughout the day. That meant there were long, painful stretches when there were ten people staring at us in a field built for nearly a thousand. It was embarrassingly empty. The failure of our dream was laid bare for everyone to see. And by everyone, I mean 150 people. *Maybe* 150 people.

Charlie Hall did his best to encourage us with a pep talk. He told us that what we were doing was still important in the kingdom and that on a spiritual level we had no idea the kind of impact we had made. He was right, of course. We all nodded our heads and smiled, but in the end, the event failed to meet even our lowest expectations. I felt painfully low as we cleaned up the field that night. I packed up wanting desperately for the night to be over.

The next day, I woke up with an emotional hangover and vowed never to do a live event like that again.

Strike one.

Second Swing

Nearly ten years after strike one, I broke my vow and dared to venture out into the unknown waters of pursuing my dream again.

I met a fellow dreamer and entrepreneur who knew how to get money together for events. I knew how to add the passion and creativity, and so it seemed as if we were a great combo. I often flew out to Dallas so we could talk about producing a myriad of worship-centered events together. I was encouraged that we seemed to be on the same wavelength. We were both talking the same anything-is-possible sort of language. And soon we began planning a series of worship events. That summer, we officially launched our first event.

It was another outdoor venue, this time a high school parking lot just outside Dallas. As the big day approached, my anticipation grew—and so did my anxiety. Scenes of my first event flashed through my head. *What if nobody shows up? What if this is just another huge letdown?* But as I looked outside and saw people lining up, I knew this event would be different. And it was.

Thousands turned out and we sold every ticket. Even though we had to evacuate twice because of severe thunderstorms, it was a great night. I had never felt so close to seeing God's dream for me take off. It was my first taste of an event that unified worship artists, and it struck a chord deep down. Getting to this point had felt so haphazard, but its significance in my life was undeniable. Honestly, it was more than I could appreciate at the time.

I was riding high. We had the wind at our backs and soon began dreaming of an even bigger night. More artists. More people. More vision. Just all around *more.*

A few months after our first event, we visited a baseball field in Dallas that looked like a perfect venue. We met with local church leaders, promoters, and radio stations. Everything came together, and quickly.

We were about a month out from the event when a new dream hit me like a bolt of lightning. It made so much sense. We had to take these events on the road. God was doing so much already, and I longed to see that impact grow. I was ready to go all out on this thing, and a tour was the way to do it. I was convinced.

But I knew that for it to work, it had to work financially too.

I had to be able to pitch this to the powers that be in a way that made sense to them. In a business sense, we risked everything when we did a single event. Each one was make-or-break. What we needed to do was spread out the risk over multiple events. Not only that, but we needed to take a worship night to more places, not only Texas.

My passion bubbled up. My vision took shape. I was ready.

I picked up the phone and two days later found myself on a plane to Dallas to pitch the idea to investors. On the plane I frantically wrote notes detailing what these events would look like and what the tour would be called. After we met and threw around some ideas, I wrote up a budget and a plan for a worship tour that would encourage the local church—sound familiar?— and impact the community.

I was psyched, and ready. After the failure of strike one, everything was looking much better this time around.

Fast forward to the night of our second event, and I'm sitting in my temporary office trying not to hear the heated arguments about money in the room next door. I was in shock. Things had been going so well—what happened? Vision and planning for the tour was in full swing. But as the argument next door escalated, I quickly realized something—we had no money. Then it hit me that I had no hotel that night and no flight home. Even worse, I was pretty sure I wasn't going to get paid. This was getting worse by the second.

That night, I slept for three hours in a seedy hotel and then flew home before the sun was up. Needless to say, that tour never happened.

The guy I had been working with couldn't pay the expenses and dropped off the face of the earth. I couldn't reach him anymore.

Everything I had planned and dreamed about evaporated. All the hope I'd felt just twenty-four hours before was gone.

Later, I found out that the guy went to prison for tax evasion. Yikes. Strike two was a doozy.

Third Swing

After the letdown of two major strikes, I stepped up for my third swing. I met a guy named Shane Quick when the two of us worked on a conference for David Crowder. I did design and art for the conference, and he promoted it. The conference was called Crowder's Fantastical Church Music Conference—quintessential David Crowder titling right there—in Waco, Texas. I had been working with David for a few years, but this was my first time working with Shane.

The conference went great, and it really impacted me, not because of what was said but because of the diversity of the bands and speakers who participated. David had everybody he knew involved in it. All of them being together on one stage made a big impact on me—and later I found out it also made a big impact on Shane.

Shortly after the conference, Shane called me. He wanted to see whether I could help him with some of the creative content for a potential worship leader conference called OUTCRY. That began a conversation that lasted for years.

We had moments when we almost launched it, but the timing wasn't right. We even declined millions of dollars to do it on Coachella grounds. There were many ups and downs and redefinitions along the way, but finally we decided that OUTCRY was a tour, not a one-off event. Our vision was to have a tour dedicated to building up and encouraging local church leaders and attendees.

And just like that, swing three was a hit. Bat met ball, and our dream sailed high into the air.

Even though it was amazing to see our dream take flight, there was one night on the tour that surprised me. And it was a feeling I didn't expect.

We were in Washington, DC, and had the largest crowd I had ever seen. Twenty thousand people showed up, and we had to expand the outdoor venue to its max. The crowd was pumped; we were pumped. It was an amazing night. But it was also one of the hardest nights of my life.

Our production crew was bogged down with technical issues. There were also a lot of interpersonal problems on the team. And on top of the work challenges, my kids had a particularly hard day and missed their Daddy. I ended up in tears multiple times.

Then I went on stage and spoke. Did I mention there were twenty thousand people there? It should have been the highlight of my life. It should have felt amazing. But deep down I was plagued by this one nagging thought: *Tonight feels utterly and unexpectedly normal.* And by normal, I meant not at all what I wanted or expected.

I had built up expectations about what this moment would be like. I expected it to feel amazing. I expected to feel as I imagined my heroes felt. I expected it to feel like emotional fireworks. Instead, it felt unremarkable. Then I wondered, *Is "normal" what my heroes actually feel? Maybe the hype of a big crowd can't sustain or fulfill me after all? Does this feel normal because it is my new normal?*

As I stood on that stage, exhausted and spent, I realized that the only reason I was there was because this was my calling. I knew it from the time I was young. And now, as with any other job or calling, I needed to be filled up by God—and by him alone.

I know it sounds basic—Christian Life 101—but until I stood on that stage, I didn't fully understand it.

Being on tour had become as normal as a Sunday morning for me—a day in the office. Without realizing it, I'd developed an unhealthy expectation. I had a mindset that said, *Ryan, having big crowds will fulfill you. When you finally get to do events that match the size of your heroes' events—then you'll be happy. And satisfied.* Expectation swing, expectation miss.

This was a setback I wasn't anticipating—an internal one based on a failed expectation. And this failed expectation was based on comparison to other people. I had to confront the fact that my life and my journey would not look like anyone else's and that my calling was going to look, sound, and feel different from anything I imagined happening in other people's lives. I had to deal with my unhealthy expectations.

UNHEALTHY EXPECTATIONS

When our son Toby was two and our daughter Adyn was five months old, Blake took a parenting class. We were completely green and were desperate for some wise insight! Every time she came home from class, Blake shared the best tidbits she had learned that day. Out of everything she shared, one tidbit really stuck with me. It was a catchphrase her teacher used: "Expectations kill relationships."

The principle was this: if you enter a toy store with your two-year-old and expect your child to be a little angel, you are in trouble. If you expect maturity from a two-year-old, you will react with shock and anger when they inevitably start throwing a massive tantrum because they can't take every toy home with them. You won't be prepared for the onslaught of insanity that one little human can unleash on you, and your emotional reaction will harm your relationship with your child. But if you have a realistic and proper expectation of your two-year-old, you will be prepared for the moments your child throws a fit—which are as sure to come as death and taxes—and you'll have a plan to deal with it.

Unhealthy expectations kill relationships.

They can also kill dreams. And there are two unhealthy expectations virtually every dreamer needs to prepare for—comparison and judgment.

Comparison

These days it's easy to compare your "behind the scenes" with the "highlight reels" of someone else's life. Social media is full of highlight-reel posts, the kind that portray the best of ourselves for all to see. This is natural and to be expected, but when you compare your seemingly mundane life with what you see online, you will inevitably feel let down.

This comparison game hits even harder when pursuing your dreams. Maybe you dream of doing big events or starting a big organization. You have heroes you look to for inspiration—entrepreneurs, big churches, creative thinkers, or TED speakers. You consume every post on their social media platforms and every video on their YouTube channels. You get a filtered snapshot summary of their life or work, and somewhere deep down you determine that this is what you want for yourself. Their life and journey are what you want for your own life. This choice may or may not be a conscious one. It may happen far beneath the surface of your awareness.

However it happens, when someone else's calling is the primary motivation for tackling your dream, your future will be laced with disappointment. And your fall after a setback will be a long one. You will be unprepared for the letdown of realizing that what you thought would fulfill you doesn't actually fulfill you—because it's based on someone else's calling rather than your own. Then giving up on your dream is easy because cynicism after disappointment is the fruit of unrealistic expectations.

But if you approach your dreams with healthy expectations—knowing that all of it won't be sunshine and lollipops—you are far less likely to give up when the setbacks come. You are far less likely to be ungrateful when you see your dream come to fruition. And you will be far more likely to keep dreaming and pursuing until you get to a point that exceeds your original dream.

Your life will not look like your hero's life. That's okay. Your life will likely feel normal and ordinary compared with the polished, filtered life of someone else. But that doesn't mean their calling is better. Nor does it mean that your life is unremarkable. Remember, no other life on earth throughout all the generations looks like yours. And that is beautiful beyond words. And when you compare *that* with an Instagram post, it seems a whole lot more wonderful and miraculous.

I can guarantee you this: the moment a big dream of yours comes to pass, you will realize that it doesn't *feel* like you thought. And you will also realize that the way you treated the seemingly mundane aspects of your life up to that point is how you will treat your dream. If you took your life for granted up to that point, you won't miraculously appreciate whatever your life becomes after your dream comes true.

So stop comparing yourself and setting your expectations on

things that aren't real. Start to look at your life with appreciation for what it is right now. Gratitude and confidence in your uniqueness are strong medicine for unhealthy expectations.

Judgment

When we engage in comparison, we typically feel down on ourselves because we compare the worst in ourselves with the best in others. But there's a flip side to unrealistic expectations that happens when we do the opposite. Comparing the best in ourselves to the less-than-best in others is a little thing called judgment. Judgment tells you that your giftings and convictions are better than the giftings and convictions of someone else. It's a self-righteous mentality that ultimately harms you as much as it harms others.

And social media makes judgment as easy to do as comparison. It's easy to hurl insults at others from a seemingly safe digital distance. We can judge someone else's religious or political beliefs with ease. We love to grab sound bites and out-of-context quotes and throw shade on the beliefs, motives, and choices of someone else.

The unhealthy expectation here is the lie that says everyone else should share our values, our philosophies, and our convictions. We measure other people's lives to our own and nearly always find them lacking or less-than. Worse, we assume we understand their motives and pass judgment on those as well. The irony is that many of us remain completely unaware of our own motives.

The deep-down of our soul is searched and known by God and God alone. God is the only one who takes the sum of our past and weaves it with the knowledge of our future to reveal the true motives of the heart. That is why David wrote:

Search me, God, and know my heart;
    test me and know my anxious thoughts.
See if there is any offensive way in me,
    and lead me in the way everlasting. (Psalm 139:23–24)

If we are being completely honest, we can barely assess what's in our own hearts, let alone the heart of someone else. David needed God to search his heart and motives, and so do we.

In society these days, we conflate accountability and judgment. Accountability is the thing you exercise with those you know. Judgment is accountability extended where there is no authority. So if you think your job is to call out that well-known speaker on social media, I have news for you. It isn't. That preacher or leader has his or her own friends who are responsible for keeping them accountable.

Jesus said in Matthew 7:2 that the measure by which we judge someone else is the measure by which we are judged in return. Even on social media. So if you are quick with the judgment stick on an out-of-context sound bite, don't be surprised if it comes back to you! We need to grow in our empathy and grace for one another. We need to pour honor out on fellow Christians who are making a big impact. In Romans 12:10 (ESV) Paul told us to "outdo one another in showing honor." We need to compete on how gracefully we pour honor on one another.

This is crucial for the dreamer. Don't waste time trying to keep strangers accountable through judgment. One day that influential leader may be you. Instead, outdo everyone in how much you honor and value those around you. *Real* influencers start there.

UNITY

Unity is perhaps the most powerful antidote to the unhealthy expectations of comparison and judgment. It's hard to envy another person's life when we are in proximity to his or her mess. It's harder to judge the motives of someone when we're close to them. The closer we get to someone, the more we realize that their life is both more approachable and more complicated than we knew.

This is why Jesus prayed for us to have unity.

> My prayer is not for them alone. I pray also for those who will believe in me through their message, that all of them may be one, Father, just as you are in me and I am in you. May they also be in us so that the world may believe that you have sent me. I have given them the glory that you gave me, that they may be one as we are one—I in them and you in me—so that they may be brought to complete unity. Then the world will know that you sent me and have loved them even as you have loved me. (John 17:20–23)

Jesus says the world will know us because of our loving unity. He prayed that our oneness would be the same as that between him and the Father. To tackle comparison and judgment in our lives, we need to see each other as Jesus sees us. And we need to love and think the best of one another, just as we need to be able to love and think the best about ourselves.

You may be wondering, *What happened there, Ryan? How did we go from talking about setbacks to talking about comparison, judgment, and now unity?*

Welcome to the tangle of pictures and newspaper clippings connected by pins and strings that is my mind. (Insert eye-roll emoji.)

I'm going back to my initial premise. Setbacks are real, and they will happen to you. There is no "maybe" about it. And the health of your expectations going in will determine the depths to which you fall post-setback. These expectations are fueled and formed in one place—your desire, or coveting, of what you perceive about someone else's life.

Ultimately, the setback itself is not the real danger; it's your *reaction* to the setback that can derail you. Your mindset and how healthy your expectations are determine the speed with which you bounce back—if you do bounce back.

If you are currently pre-setback and everything is sunshine and lollipops, you need to begin checking your motives and expectations now. The spoiler alert is this: seeing your dream take off will be amazing, but there will be a crash at some point. You have been warned.

Identity is also key. Go back to chapter 3 to refresh if you need to. You are not your dream. Your dream is entrusted to you by God. It is an aspect of you that will be amazing in some seasons and bland in other seasons. But if your identity is grounded in Jesus, the depth and length of your fall will be greatly diminished when the setback comes.

✧ ✧

Okay. We've laid the foundation. We've tackled the dream killers. Now we're ready to start. Please keep your arms and legs inside the vehicle at all times because this is going to be a wild ride.

PART 3

START

CHAPTER 8

WORK

Let's dive into my favorite thing. *Starting.*

First things first. Your dream is going to require work. Hard work. *Years* of hard work. I know this isn't a big applause line or something you may be rushing off to quote on social media, but it's the place we need to start.

Sadly, I have come across many well-meaning Christians who think hard work is "striving," not relying on God, or that it somehow negates the work of the Holy Spirit. I know people who have been waiting on a promise God gave them years ago but have never considered the opportunities God has already placed in their lives. But there is work to do *today* on the promises of yesterday.

KABASH YOUR DREAMS

Let's revisit the Genesis passage we talked about in chapter 3. That's where we explored work as our calling to *subdue*—to use our gifts, talents, and hands to make something beautiful out of the resources in front of us.

> And God blessed them. And God said to them, "Be fruitful and multiply and fill the earth and subdue it, and have

dominion over the fish of the sea and over the birds of the heavens and over every living thing that moves on the earth." (Genesis 1:28 ESV)

The Hebrew word translated "subdue" is *kabash*. It means to subject, subdue, force, or keep under. This is the work God has called us to do. And it's important to know that this isn't the cursed work that happened after the fall (Genesis 3); this is the pure work God gives us because we are made in his image—our calling is to be fruitful and exercise dominion.

This is work as it was meant to be—joyful and purposeful. It carries proper rhythm and regular Sabbath. But it is work nonetheless. And if you think it's optional or something that doesn't have any bearing on you spiritually, you are mistaken. When you *kabash* the world around you, there will be sweat on your brow. There will be tension and resistance. There will be nights you fall into bed exhausted and spent. But all that work leads to the deep and life-giving creation of something new— something that's unique to you. It will be something you can look back on and smile at, knowing that God used you to change one thing here on earth, something that brings a little more of God's kingdom here on earth as it is in heaven.

✧ ✧

A few weekends ago, I was enjoying a beautiful and relaxed Saturday morning at my son's football game when I ran into an acquaintance I hadn't seen in a while. We were catching up when he dropped a conversational bomb. You know, that moment when someone says something you fundamentally disagree with, but you have to pause to decide whether you want to get into an argument. Which is to say, it was the moment my beautiful and relaxed Saturday morning was crashed with an awkward disagreement.

"You know the beautiful thing about Jesus?" he said, "It's that you don't have to do anything. You just have to be with him. That's all that really matters. That's what he taught us. I mean, look at Mary and Martha . . . [insert monologue about not 'striving' and 'just being' for Jesus]."

We've already worked through the story about Mary and Martha, but as a recap, I don't believe the point of what Jesus said to Martha is "Work bad. Sitting good." We only have to look at Genesis to see that we are called to dominate our work, not have our work dominate us. Martha was allowing her work to dominate her, to distract her from something greater—the better portion. If you and I allow work to steal our greater moments—the ones with God or the people in our lives—then we are allowing work to dominate us. Okay, you already know that. Moving on.

But these were the thoughts that hit me. Suddenly, I had a logjam in my brain. I had so many rebuttals hit me at once that I froze. I couldn't possibly dive into all the depths of this topic and still watch my son play. So I opted for the cowardly way out. I simply smiled and nodded, returning my attention to the game. I probably stumbled through an inane response to change the subject. "Hmmm, it's a pretty good point. . . . But how 'bout the receiving in this game? They sure are catching it, huh?"

Okay. I knew that what my friend was saying may have sounded right, but it's a misguided understanding that has unfortunately spread throughout Christian culture. It's the view that God does it all while I sit back and wait for my ship to roll in.

If I don't like my current job or my boss isn't nice to me, then God promptly "calls me somewhere else." This was the gist of what my friend was saying that day.

What he conveniently forgot was a story Jesus told called the parable of the talents. In the story, a master divvies out investment money—referred to as "talents"—to three servants. The first servant receives five talents, the second receives two, and the third receives one. It wasn't an even-sum game. Jesus points out that the master distributed the talents according to the servants' "ability."

Then the master goes on a journey. He doesn't tell the servants what to do with the talents; he simply entrusts his property to them and then leaves town. For a long time.

All the servants seem to understand the character of their master, because they know the master expects them to invest what they've been given. So they get busy, work hard, and take some risks to multiply their talents—all of them, that is, except one. This servant chooses to avoid all risk and buries his talent instead. He doesn't even put it in a bank. He simply buries it in his backyard. Chances are that nobody in his life even knew he had it. He didn't think about *its* potential or *his* potential to make more. He simply and fearfully kept it hidden. He kept it safe.

The problem?

The master didn't want his investment to be kept safe. He wanted it to be invested. He wanted it multiplied. He wanted it risked for the expansion of his influence.

When the master returns from his journey, he systematically interviews his servants to find out how they did with their investments. He goes to the first servant, and this is how the conversation goes:

"He who had received the five talents came forward, bringing five talents more, saying, 'Master, you delivered to me five talents; here, I have made five talents more.' His master said to him, 'Well done, good and faithful servant. You have been faithful over a little; I will set you over much. Enter into the joy of your master.'" (Matthew 25:20–21 ESV)

The master commends the servant for investing and doubling his investment. He says he will now entrust him with more. He says this same thing to the servant who'd been given two talents. Then it's the third servant's turn.

"He also who had received the one talent came forward, saying, 'Master, I knew you to be a hard man, reaping where you did not sow, and gathering where you scattered no seed, so I was afraid, and I went and hid your talent in the ground. Here, you have what is yours.' But his master answered him, 'You wicked and slothful servant! You knew that I reap where I have not sown and gather where I scattered no seed? Then you ought to have invested my money with the bankers, and at my coming I should have received what was my own with interest. So take the talent from him and give it to him who has the ten talents.'" (Matthew 25:24–28 ESV)

I know—harsh. But we need to pay attention to what Jesus is saying. Keep in mind that this is the same Jesus who also said, "My yoke is easy and my burden is light" (Matthew 11:30) and who commended Mary for choosing the better portion when she spent time with him rather than working. He's not a tyrant. He is loving and kind and understanding. But Jesus makes it clear that his investment in us comes with *accountability*. God really does want a return on his investment. If we invest whatever it is he has given us, we will see it grow, and then he will entrust us with more. But if we instead bury whatever he has given us, he will take it away. Fearfully hiding his investment makes us poor stewards of that investment.

And yet some of us choose that path—we bury the influence and talents we have been given. While we claim to "wait" on God, our God-given dreams sit dormant. The fields of opportunity where we could be reaping a harvest lie barren. The deep-down, God-woven parts of our lives remain buried, and not even our closest friends or family know they're there.

But why? Why are we so prone to do this?

Many of us do it in the name of "humility." We don't want to "make much of ourselves." Or we feel a compulsion to say "it's not about us, it's about him" as we point to the sky. We have a lot of Christian lingo we wrap around it.

But I believe it's fear, not humility, that holds you back. Fear tells you not to try. Fear makes you second-guess your every move. Fear reminds you of what you aren't. Fake humility causes you to hold back, second-guess your every move, and constantly return to your weaknesses. It's a "humility" that beats you down and never lets you shine.

True humility originates in confidence—confidence in who God is and who he created you to be. It's an understanding that God gave you gifts that are not your own. They came from him, and he expects you to use them. As a result, you should be confident in using your gifts because you are confident in the Gift Giver.

When you operate from true humility, you understand that

God has also given everyone around you their own unique gift set, which means you don't have to feel threatened or intimidated by other people's gifts. Instead, you want them to use their gifts, and your confidence in God results in more love and support for those around you.

Do you see what's happening here? Confidence leads to humility.

Let me say it another way. Let's say you have a leadership gift. As you step out in more confidence with your leadership, you will begin to see clearly the beauty and power of the Gift Giver. As you do this, others will see the imprint of the Gift Giver on you and be encouraged to step out in more confidence with their own gifts—because freedom begets freedom. And as you see them step out, you will be even more amazed by the diversity of gifts that the Gift Giver brings!

Whew . . .

You may be getting dizzy with my logic at this point, but here's the bottom line: God's name is not glorified when we fearfully hide our gifts. Having influence and stewarding our gifts well is hard work. It requires time and energy. But when we do it with our eyes on Jesus—the Gift Giver—and it is done with the goal of expanding his kingdom, it will yield a return on what he invested in us. And when that happens, your influence expands, and your gifts are honed and strengthened.

God has given you everything you need to pursue your dream. The talents, resources, connections—everything. And what you do with the little or much in your hands right now will determine how much more God will give you tomorrow.

Okay, so we've established that work and confidence are needed to get your dream off the ground. But let's dive into some ways you can start working on your dream today—some things that will kickstart you into *kabashing* your God-given dream.

GET A PLAN

In my early twenties, I was convinced I wanted to be a recording artist. I had been a worship leader for a while and was writing a lot of original music—music my mom thought was great, by the way. After working on some indie albums, I was ready to take on the world, but I couldn't seem to get any traction on my music and was feeling desperate to make something happen.

One day I met someone who had the resources and connections to put me on tour. My dream at the time was to take my original music on the road, and this was my ticket. This was the break I had been waiting for! I sucked up all my courage and called him one day. "I want you to send me on tour," I said point-blank.

He laughed and said, "I'd love to send you on tour. What are you working on?"

"I'm in the middle of working on a couple of EPs," I said, "I'm pretty excited about them."

"Can you send them to me?" he asked.

This took me by surprise. Couldn't he take my word for it? I felt a little squirmy because these EPs I felt pretty excited about were far from done. Maybe they weren't even started.

"I'm not quite finished with them," I said, trying to buy some time. Then he asked more questions about my plans to get them done. Did I have a budget? Or a producer? The more questions he asked, the fewer answers I had. The conversation eventually stalled. Then he said something I'll never forget.

"Ryan, you have to give me something I can say yes or no to."

That's what he said, but I got the message behind the words, which went something like this: *You aren't as prepared as you think, and just asking to go on tour isn't enough. You need to have a plan I can get on board with, and you need to prove to me that you are a good investment—someone worth taking a risk on.*

I got off the phone feeling both embarrassed and determined. I was embarrassed that I had essentially wasted a great opportunity—that of course I'd already shared with all my friends. But I also felt determined to work hard and to do my homework next time. I vowed never to waste another opportunity because I didn't have a well-thought-out plan.

WRITE IT DOWN

And the LORD answered me:

> "Write the vision;
> > make it plain on tablets,
> > so he may run who reads it.
> For still the vision awaits its appointed time;
> > it hastens to the end—it will not lie.
> If it seems slow, wait for it;
> > it will surely come; it will not delay.
> > (Habakkuk 2:2–3 ESV)

These have always been central verses in my life. Whether I'm leading or supporting someone else's vision, I always use this as a metric for vision casting. Write it down. Make it plain. Clarity is everything.

The team I lead knows that I like to have a plan. I like to know what the goals are, what the vision is, and what the metrics are that we will use to determine whether the project is a win. My team and I need a plan that helps us see the vision clearly. And I like to see that vision on paper. I don't mean that figuratively. I mean I like to see it on physical paper. I know we live in the twenty-first century and we can plan digitally, but I like to have my plans in my hand. It helps me to feel that whatever is being proposed is more concrete, especially in the early stages.

I also like having a plan on paper because it forces me to edit. Holding five pages of single-spaced, ten-point text in your hand during a meeting is overwhelming. As far as I'm concerned, a plan needs to fit on one page. If I hand it to someone, I want that person to be able to read it in thirty seconds. Why? Because succinct communication is effective, and effective communication is the most important step in getting a dream or vision off the ground. In the business world, the thirty-second summary is called an elevator pitch—a pitch short enough to be communicated in the duration of an elevator ride. And it's deceptively difficult to pull off. The shorter the pitch, the more work is required. Each and every word counts.

A member of President Woodrow Wilson's cabinet once asked him how long it took him to prepare a speech. "It depends," he replied. "If I am to speak ten minutes, I need a week for preparation; if fifteen minutes, three days; if half an hour, two days; if an hour, I am ready now."[1] *Exactly.*

Creating a plan and pitching it requires a lot of preparation. When I am pitching a vision or dream, I always focus on four things—why, how, time frame, and budget. There may be additional things specific to your dream that you will need to address, but these four should give you a good framework to start with.

Why?

Simon Sinek is an author and organizational consultant who gave an influential TED Talk titled "How Great Leaders Inspire Action." He later wrote a book about it called *Start with Why*. In it, he says, "Very few people or companies can clearly articulate WHY they do WHAT they do. . . . By WHY I mean what is your purpose, cause or belief? WHY does your company exist? WHY do you get out of bed every morning? And WHY should anyone care? . . . People don't buy WHAT you do, they buy WHY you do it."[2]

Now, maybe you own a business, maybe you don't. But the importance of this for launching your dream can't be overstated. Why do you want to do what you are dreaming about? Why does it wake you up in the middle of the night? Why do you believe in it?

As I began my walk toward OUTCRY, the why question nagged at me. Going on tour was not a *why*, it was a *what*. After considerable digging and talking and praying, the why of OUTCRY eventually emerged: *we want to champion the church*. A lot of people were focused on the imperfections of the church, and we wanted to counter that. We wanted to remind people of how important the church was to Jesus and how it's still the greatest movement in history.

That's it. That was the why of OUTCRY. It still is.

Now, obviously, I had a longer version of the vision statement that eventually filled an entire book, and reducing that down to a sentence wasn't easy. In fact, it took months to boil it down. But the work was worth it because it's been a powerful compass for us.

This is the first step in crafting a plan with a strong vision. Get your why boiled down to one or two sentences. Write down the longer version first and then start editing it down to its essence. And don't assume everyone knows what you know. Check your assumptions. Try to get outside yourself to articulate your vision in a way other people will readily understand. Once you boil it down, ask people for feedback—including people who don't know you. If the feedback indicates that the vision is unclear, hit the drawing board again until it's clear.

Then take your cleaned-up vision statement and put it on the top of your plan under the bold heading, *Why?*

How?

The next part of your plan answers the question *How?* This is when you dive into the nuts and bolts of your vision. These are the thoughts that probably keep you up at night. How are you going to get this off the ground? Logistics. Tactics. Strategies. These can fill ten pages if you aren't careful. But the goal is to get it down to four or five bullet points.

For example, on OUTCRY our "how" ebbs and flows, but they will generally be something like this:

1. Talk to (insert organization) about raising our sponsorship budget this year.
2. Secure our production/design teams by talking to (insert name).
3. Ryan will create a stronger all-artist intro/outro for the night.
4. (insert name) is working on an updated budget and is trimming 15 percent.
5. (insert name) will create a stronger preannouncement strategy for social media.

These are a couple of general examples. Most likely you would be writing about something different. But notice how I try to keep it general while addressing some sort of action step. I try to hit all the high points and address the things I think the powers that be will want to know.

A few years ago, my team at church threw around an idea for a worship conference in Phoenix. We boiled down our vision and had a fairly strong why. We also identified some strategies, but when it came time to pitch the conference to the powers that be, their how questions were different from ours. We had been focused on how to make the conference heartfelt and creative, but they wanted to know how we were going to *sell* it. They wanted to make sure we mitigated our financial risks.

The more questions they asked, the less confidence I had in my answers. Even though our team had talked at length about our how, we hadn't boiled it down to a few bullet points. As a result, I felt unfocused and scattered trying to answer their questions. I felt as if I got a pass, but by the skin of my teeth. In the end they gave us a cautious thumbs up, but I left that meeting resolved to follow two principles the next time I needed to articulate the "how" of a vision.

Principle 1: Know your audience. Anticipate the perspective of the powers that be. What's most important to them? Do they want to know more about the heart of the vision or how you're going to finance it? Do they want detail or broad strokes? Do they come from a business background? Did they go to art school or seminary? Put yourself in their shoes, and try to anticipate their main concerns.

Don't expect them to care about your vision. Don't lose patience when you need to explain it for the one thousandth time. These are unique individuals, just as you are, and they may not see the world as you do. So do your research, and get to know your audience. Then work hard to communicate your vision in a way that respects and honors their perspectives.

Principle 2: Be prepared. I tend to do my best thinking in the shower. I don't know why. Maybe it's the warm water or that, given my crazy life, it's one of the few times I have a moment alone. Whatever the reason, showers bring out the creativity in me. I've written songs and pitched book ideas in the shower. I've planned tours and debated the theological ramifications of AI in the shower. I've planned and budgeted a hundred potential house remodels in the shower. You name it, I've planned it.

I also have conversations in the shower. Not in the creepy, in-person way—I'm not facetiming anyone or anything. These are conversations I have in my head. Often I imagine someone who disagrees with me or has a different point of view than I do, and I try to convince that person of the validity of my point of view. I get in a frenzy of conversation that leaves me lost in all the possible retorts, often ending with my wife calling out, "Ryan, are you still thinking in there?"

These shower conversations have become a form of preparation that serves me well. They help me anticipate the devil's advocate point of view and to rehearse the best responses.

As the Boy Scouts say, be prepared. You have to cover a lot of ground in your planning in order to internalize the high points of your plan. You have to walk into a meeting exuding confidence and having thought through answers to tough questions. And whether you thought them through in your office or in the shower, it really doesn't matter. As long as you are taking time to anticipate questions and sharpen your responses.

Once I get into the pitch or an important meeting, I operate by the three strikes rule. It looks like this: If I'm presenting a vision and someone asks me a question I don't know the answer to, I gracefully say, "I'm actually not sure, let me look into that." I consider that strike one in their confidence in me. If another question I can't answer comes my way, no matter how eloquent I am, that's strike two, and the person will lose more confidence in me. It's hard to bounce back after two strikes—and if there are three strikes, *fahgettaboudit*. I'm done. I need to lick my wounds, go back to the drawing board, and pray for another chance.

On your planning sheet, try to boil down your strategy to four or five bullet points, and put them under your *How?* section. But make sure you are also ready to go down any rabbit hole the person or team you are pitching to may take you down. Be prepared!

When and How Much?

Planning a time frame and budget are things people tend to fear or feel intimidated by. It feels risky to estimate a time frame and budget when you aren't 100 percent confident in your estimates. But all new endeavors have question marks around them. No matter how confident and experienced you are, if you are truly doing something new, it will surprise you with something. Things pop up no matter how prepared you are. But you can't let this deter you. You have to do your best to define what may seem undefinable. You have to set a ballpark figure so people know what to expect. Without it, you really have nothing. No one says yes to a vision without a budget. And vision that can't get a decision will ultimately lead nowhere.

When it comes to presenting the time frame and budget in

a pitch meeting, I tend to rip the Band-Aid off quickly. "This is going to take $100,000 and six to nine months to do." Even if I'm afraid of the response, the powers that be need to know, so there's no sense in soft-pedaling it.

I recently sat through someone else's pitch. He looked as though he had worked hard on it. He had a PowerPoint presentation and a lot of good insight and had done his research. He identified his frustrations and his hopes for the future. He gave some great facts to back up his philosophy, had some funny one-liners, and told a few personal stories. He had me listening and engaged. Then he stopped. The end.

I felt like saying, *"And . . . ?"* There were no measurables. There were no specifics on how he was going to pull it off or what he'd need in terms of budget to get started. There was absolutely nothing to say yes or no to. It was a great general idea for us to ponder, nothing more.

As we asked questions, his response was always, "Yeah, we could do that! Sure, we could do that too!" Instead of using the meeting to pitch his vision, he was using it as an opportunity to *brainstorm* his vision. We started drowning in the endless possibilities, and soon the conversation stalled awkwardly.

I left feeling frustrated and exhausted. He had a great idea, not a vision. An idea is something like "I want to start an international ministry" or "I want to start a business that puts people first." These are good ideas, but not visions people will jump on board with. Ideas aren't something people usually want to throw money at. A plan without measurables is just an idea. If you don't define anything in your plan, you will frustrate yourself and the people you try to pitch your vision to.

Your vision needs structure. Develop a rough time frame and

budget—and figure in more time and money than you think you might need rather than less. When you tell someone with the power to fund or propel your vision, "I want to start a school" or "I want to record an album" but have no idea what you'll need to make it happen, you're doing your vision and the other person a disservice. The conversation will most likely end with a comment along the lines of, "Okay, take some time to do some research, and think this through a bit more before we revisit this."

A vision with an undefined time frame and budget is a vision that's dead on arrival.

So do the work and develop the most realistic time frame and budget you can. Ask people that are more advanced than you in your area that can mentor you and give you advice. Research online or buy a book on the area you want to pursue. Then once you feel confident, put it in your plan, or at least have it on hand. Because if the *Why?* and the *How?* parts of your plan are strong, the next questions you'll be asked will almost certainly be, *When?* and *How much?*

✧ ✧

If you have your plan written down and ready to propose—even if you have nobody to propose it to yet—you are ahead of 90 percent of the dreamers out there. You have a concrete vision, and you are ready for the moment God brings that person along.

But that brings up the question, how do you find that person to pitch to? How do you make connections? And this brings up a question that I think is plaguing Christian dreamers everywhere: *Is it Jesuslike to promote your dream and to network strategically?*

My response? *Absolutely.*

CHAPTER 9

CONNECT

The dreamer's journey toward his or her dream must inevitably involve other people. You cannot carry your dream by yourself. You need other people to partner with you. You need investors to finance you. You need other people to relate to and support what you are diving into. If you're doing all the work, I don't think your dream will get very far. And if it does, it won't last long. Bringing people along with you is the real challenge.

This is something I become more convinced of the longer I live on this planet. Strategically connecting and stewarding influence are some of the most vital skills to hone on your journey as a dreamer. And strangely, it's also something that feels a bit taboo in Christian circles.

I was talking with someone recently who said, "The biggest problem in Christian culture today is self-promotion." Now that is a bold statement. But it triggered my little brain motor to kick on and begin a tireless search for the logic in that statement. I'm not sure I completely agree with it, but I will say this: the idea of self-promotion is not one I'm fond of. It can be taken way too far—especially in light of some of the things Jesus taught. For example: "Beware of practicing your righteousness before other people in order to be seen by them, for then you will have no reward from your Father who is in heaven" (Matthew 6:1 ESV).

And "The greatest among you will be your servant. For those who exalt themselves will be humbled, and those who humble themselves will be exalted" (Matthew 23:11–12).

We've all probably had the unpleasant experience of being around people who self-promote to excess. Maybe they're starting something new and are excited about it—or maybe they just can't stop taking selfies. Whatever it is, you can smell desperation for notoriety a mile away. It makes us uncomfortable because, let's be honest, who wants to be trapped in a conversation with someone who can't talk about anything but themselves? The excessive self-promoter accomplishes little more than driving people and opportunities away. Proverbs says it well:

> Do not put yourself forward in the king's presence
>> or stand in the place of the great,
> for it is better to be told, "Come up here,"
>> than to be put lower in the presence of a noble.
>> (Proverbs 25:6–7 ESV)

When we force ourselves forward, many times we're operating out of fear more than pride. We're performing so that those around us will be impressed and our stature will grow in their eyes. But then our self-worth rises or falls because of their approval or the number of likes we get on a post. We live off the dopamine hits we get when people follow us on social media or when we get public accolades.

This is the kind of self-promotion Jesus cautioned against. This is the self-promotion strategy that will blow up in your face. And those who get stuck in this pattern—which, let's face it, it's most of us from time-to-time—need some outside perspective.

Sometimes it's good to ask those around you about the vibe you put out on social media or even in a meeting.

✧ ✧

We have an amazing person named Tammy who works as a consultant with our church. She's strong member of our team and helps us with HR, but she also consults for firms around the country. One of the things I love most about Tammy is her honesty. I never have to wonder what she really thinks. Sometimes her honesty hits me between the eyes, but she's never unkind. She somehow manages to deliver her feedback with an eloquence and grace that leaves me feeling motivated to change rather than crushed by her critique.

A while back we had an important staff day. We were communicating about a lot of critical issues, and we had to say everything clearly and carefully. I was responsible for letting the staff know about some major decisions. I pride myself in being a clear communicator, and I usually shine when the pressure increases, so I left that meeting feeling good about how I'd done my part. There were no blowups or confrontations. I saw heads nodding, so I chalked it up as a win.

Until I stopped by Tammy's office.

I popped my head in and asked, "Hey, Tammy, how do you think it went?" I fully anticipated a positive reaction. Instead, she said, "Well, it could have gone better. You used the word 'we' a lot in that meeting. It made it feel really exclusive. Like the leadership team had solved all the problems and come up with answers without valuing input from the rest of the staff."

Boom. Mayday! Mayday!

So much for feeling good about how I'd done my part. Instead of a high five, I got an unfiltered view of how others perceived me—and it wasn't anything close to how I perceived myself. But it was a view I needed to see.

Because our view of ourselves can be wildly different from how others view or experience us, our self-perception is sometimes as accurate as the reflection in a funhouse mirror. Sometimes the things we think we did great at can be experienced very differently by those around us. We need some outside input from people we trust.

Once again, it helps to have a proper identity. With an unhealthy or misplaced identity, these sorts of critiques can be crushing. But when your identity is found in Jesus and what he says about you, honest feedback stings less. It's not completely painless, but it's much more manageable.

To avoid being "that person" who self-promotes for position and accolades, you need friends who will give you honest feedback. Honest feedback on how others experience you could shine a light on an area of your heart that is unhealthy.

When you're launching your dream, avoid being the self-promoter who drives people away and ends up killing the very thing you are trying to get off the ground. Self-promotion as a means of control or boosting your self-worth will always fail. Self-promotion as a means of growing your own kingdom and not God's will always leave you lacking. But self-promotion to foster your influence is another thing entirely.

FOSTERING YOUR INFLUENCE

Christian culture, in the Western church at least, seems to have a love-hate relationship with influence. We follow our favorite speakers, musicians, and churches, but at the same time, we're more than a little skittish about "celebrity Christians." We love influential leaders, but we get nervous when they're too influential. We have seen so many unhealthy Christian leaders crash and burn that we're wary of influence.

This dynamic often leaves a Christian leader feeling conflicted about their role. Deep down, every leader yearns for influence—*increasing* influence—on the world around them. But Christian leaders tend to keep it at arm's length in an effort to avoid the appearance of pride. They fight off the desire to "make a name" for themselves or to "build their network." Why? Because many are fearful. Fearful that they might end up operating in self-aggrandizing pride. Or even worse, that others would perceive them as having self-aggrandizing pride.

Cue the lock up. Cue the burying of dreams and passions. Cue the lack of confidence and the diminishment of influence.

But here are my main questions. The questions that keep me up at night. The questions I mull over in the shower.

Does having a good reputation and working to grow my influence diminish God's glory? Does an increase in my influence somehow decrease God's influence? Is God's desire for me to lie low and wallow, or is it to proudly display the giftings and passion he has given me?

I was recently consulting with another team about an event they were putting on. I was talking about some of the leaders I knew and throwing out names of people I could call and invite to be a part of this event. Then one of the leaders from the other team cut in and, in frustration, said, "Ryan, I want our team to have a strong influence for themselves, not just to piggy back off yours."

On the one hand, I saw where he was coming from. Sure,

I get it. Everyone wants to have relationships with influential leaders. But on the other hand, his comment felt like a punch to the gut, and it triggered a tidal wave of thoughts and emotions in me. As he spoke more, the undertone of his comment became clear. He viewed any influence I had as something that was simply bestowed on me—an unearned gift that came easy. Without cost. He believed that if God was at work in what we were doing, he would magically endow the other members of the team with the necessary relationships and connections.

His comment felt like a body blow because it was the furthest thing from the truth. The network and contacts I have now weren't simply handed to me, they were developed—over decades. I worked hard to be faithful with the influence I had each step of the way. I learned to develop a list of leaders I could connect with, but it wasn't only cold, self-serving strategy. It took heart. It took serving the dreams of others. Because ultimately, good networking is good relationship building. It's years and years of *consistent* relationship building.

To have someone downplay or trivialize this hurts. And it's a mistake.

God may bring relationships to you, but what you do with those relationships is up to you. You can develop the network and contacts you have now. The question is: How are you fostering the influence you already have?

✧ ✧

I was in my early twenties and struggling with what to do with my life. Like every other person my age, I'd done some experimenting. I had been a worship pastor for a while. I had spent some time doing foreign mission work through an organization called Youth with a Mission. My wife, Blake, and I had been married for a few years, and though I was technically an adult, I was struggling under the weight of having to "figure out my calling"—the one thing I'd do for the rest of my life, the thing that would fulfill all my desires. And I was feeling very behind.

I prayed every day. I journaled. I talked with friends and family about what I was going to do with my life. And it felt as if I hit dead end after dead end. I knew what it was like to hear God's voice and to be obedient in going where he asked me to go. But this was different. Now all I got from God was silence.

On top of all that, the church that was paying me a whopping $500 a month to be their worship pastor experienced a leadership blowup. When it came to finding my calling, I felt as if I was on a sinking ship. It was all going down, and I had no life raft.

One night my wife and I were at her parents' house having dinner. My mother-in-law and I started talking about this very subject. I told her how I hadn't heard from God. That I had been waiting and waiting, seemingly without any leading.

Then she asked me a question I honestly had not considered, an idea so simple it sounded absurd.

"So if you weren't a worship leader, what else would you like to do?"

That was novel. *What do I want to do? If I could do anything other than what I am doing, what would I do?*

After some thinking, I said, "I like photography."

Two weeks later I submitted an application for art school. Two months later I was a student in graphic design at the University of Arizona. I was plowing forward into a career I felt excited about. A career—if I'm being honest—I wasn't 100 percent sure was my calling, but a career I felt I could do. And though God had not given me a lightning bolt of revelation about my future, I soon found that it was indeed his leading into the great unknown, a leading into a story I could never have written for myself.

After a couple of years of school, it occurred to me that if I was going to make a career out of doing graphic design as a freelancer, I'd need to get a couple of high-profile clients. I'd have to start building my influence in this world.

So I did something that would soon change my life.

I wrote an email to every band and musician I could think of that went something like this:

Dear [insert musician's name],

Hi. My name is Ryan Romeo. I'm a big fan! [Insert specifics of what I love about said artist.] I wanted to send you a message about your graphic and web design. I am a web designer and graphic designer, and I'd love the opportunity to work for you! I know you're probably super busy, but please let me know if I could ever work some ideas up for you!

Thanks!

Ryan

After a week of sending out emails, I got only one response:

If you come up with some ideas, we'd be glad to look at them.

David Crowder

I couldn't believe it. David was my hero, and he responded to me! Okay, fine, his response was a nondescript, noncommittal statement geared to be a polite response to a bold request by a complete stranger. I see that now. But at the time, it was an open door. It was a wide-open door. It was a foregone conclusion. In my mind, I was practically working for David Crowder!

I just needed to do the work.

I took the next week to work up website ideas. I dove into Flash design—before Steve Jobs declared Flash dead—and began working up an animated website. I just needed something to keep me focused. So as I dove in, I gave myself a one-week deadline. Looking back, it was insanely tight, but I was aware that since I had David Crowder's attention, I needed to strike while the iron was hot. Every night I worked until three o'clock in the morning teaching myself website coding. I scoured online forums and copied and pasted code. I learned how to host a website (which was way more involved back then) and how to animate frame-by-frame.

At the end of one week, I had two ideas—one that I loved and another one I made as insurance. And with a load of butterflies in my stomach, I closed my eyes and hit the send button.

Two weeks later I was officially working on a new website for the David Crowder Band. From that moment on, things took off for me.

I met new people and forged new relationships. And each relationship was one I felt called to steward. I felt my influence growing, and with it my sense of responsibility. I knew that God had made the initial connections for me, but what I did with those connections was something for which I alone had responsibility.

From that point on, I did my best to be intentional about fostering and stewarding my influence. I've learned some principles that I hope will help guide you. Let's dive into some practical stuff. These are short insights that will help you care for your relationships with others and expand the influence in your life.

Be a Servant

It's not enough to know someone; you have to serve them. It's not enough to have a connection to someone; you have to love them and care for them. Only from that servant posture will your influence grow. So take some time to figure out how you can serve them.

Maybe there are people of influence you want to reach out to and connect with. Nowadays, that is easier than ever. But don't be creepy and send them a portrait you painted of their Twitter profile pic or a song you wrote for them—all things I've seen people do, by the way. Do something simple! Quote them on social media. Or reach out when they're in your neck of the woods to volunteer for them. People who serve gain more influence than people who try to force their way to the spotlight.

Treat Them as Humans

People of influence are just like you. They second-guess themselves and question their impact from time to time. They have good days and bad days. *So treat them that way.* Take a minute to write them an encouraging email or message. Tell them how their work or their leadership has changed your life. You never know what a simple, honest note of encouragement can do.

Be Slow to Ask

When you connect with someone of influence, be careful and slow to ask them for a favor. And don't let your first interaction with them be to ask them to work for you somehow. Don't let your first interaction with them be for them to use their influence to benefit you. I've received many messages over the years that say something like this: "Ryan, I love the ministry that you are doing! Would you mind sharing what I'm doing on social media? Or maybe mention me from the stage?" Now, I'm sure many of these people are doing amazing things, and my heart truly and honestly goes out to them. But I don't know them at all! Some people send me messages that they are praying for me, or they take some time to encourage me or ask me for my insight on a subject. These are the people I try to take time to sit down and respond to. These are the people I connect with.

Be Consistent and Regular

There's an art to this one. I have overused this in the past, and it can result in a burned bridge. But don't be afraid to reach out to someone multiple times. If you have built a relational bridge with someone and served their dream for a time and you have deemed it time to ask them for a favor, don't be afraid to ask multiple times. They are probably very busy, and their lack of response is not necessarily an indication that they're avoiding you.

But be careful of your tone in follow-up emails or messages. Follow this outline:

- Apologize if you're bugging them: "I'm so sorry to be a pest!"
- Acknowledge that they're busy: "I know you are probably super busy."
- Ask your favor again.
- Follow up with understanding: "If this favor is too much, I completely understand! Forget I asked!"

Before you hit send, scan your email for any hints of entitlement or frustration. These will only shut down the person you are talking to. Make sure the attitude in your message—or in person—conveys humility and gives them the opportunity to say no. Why? Because if their answer is no and you passive aggressively pressure them, they will begin to ignore you, and your relational bridge will burn as if it's made of gasoline-soaked pine needles.

You are not entitled to favors from people. You are not entitled to someone making all your dreams come true. The person from whom you are asking for help is a human being, not your servant. Treat them that way.

Know When to Stop

If you have asked your person three times and there has been no response, set aside your request for now. Maybe this isn't the time. Or maybe the relational bridge isn't as strong as you thought. It's okay! Put that request on the shelf, and ask God for insight on *who* to ask next. Remember, God is more committed to the dream he placed in your heart than you are. Roadblocks in relationships have purpose just as much as connections. So pay attention to the roadblocks and know when to back off of a door you are trying to force open.

There Is No Small Connection

Here's the key principle you need to follow: "Whatever you do, work at it with all your heart, as working for the Lord, not for human masters, since you know that you will receive an inheritance from the Lord as a reward. It is the Lord Christ you are serving" (Colossians 3:23–24).

The principle of doing *everything* as working for the Lord will change how you treat the here and now. If you treat the seemingly unimportant connections in your life as if they were important, and you do this consistently, you will find that they truly are important.

You must consider every connection, every person, in your life as important—because they are. Every human God puts in your path is infinitely valuable. And how you treat that infinitely valuable connection matters. If you don't love the people around you and instead essentially treat them as stepping-stones to advance yourself, it will catch up to you. You will be running on your own strength, not the anointing of God, and you will have failed Jesus's commandment to "love your neighbor as yourself" (Matthew 22:39).

I started networking and fostering my influence from Tucson, Arizona, a small city that's practically in Mexico. It isn't the place you move to if you want to be a mover and shaker in the Christian music world. But I had two things going for me. First, God was behind it. I did the audit and consistently heard from the Lord that I would be a part of that world. Naively or not, I believed that if God was for my dream, nothing could stand against it—not even Tucson, Arizona.

Second, and equally important, I treated every connection as if it mattered. I didn't just fake it but *believed* in it. When your heart leans in to the people around you, they feel it. You feel it.

Start asking yourself a few questions:

1. What relationships do I already have that I can start leaning into more?
2. Who can I take out to lunch or coffee so I can learn more about what they know?
3. Who in my life has a dream they are working on that I can serve?

The names that come to mind when you answer these questions are the people with whom you should foster relationships. These are the people you should network with. And if you serve them, treat them as human beings, and are slow to ask them for things, they may turn into authentic friendships. Friendships lead to more friendships and an increase in influence.

I believe networking and gaining influence are great things. Doing those things isn't being prideful. It isn't cutting God out. You can network with a heart for God. And you can avoid networking because of pride and wrong motives. Let's not make this too complicated! Networking isn't pride. Pride is pride. Networking is networking.

SELF-PROMOTION THROUGH THE LENS OF A FATHER

A few years back, my daughter Adyn (pronounced add-in, as in addin' and subtractin') brought home a picture she had drawn for me in school. It was a picture of the two of us holding hands under a rainbow and smiling. Every time one of my kids bring home a picture like that, it wrecks me. I proudly displayed this particular drawing on the fridge, not because it was perfectly executed but because it was an expression of Adyn's heartfelt affection for me.

But let's imagine that the picture scenario had gone a little differently. Let's say that before bringing the picture home, Adyn decided to walk around and show it to all her classmates. With joy on her face and pride in her work, she showed off the picture she drew of herself and her daddy. And let's say I happened to walk in and see her doing this. Would I run up to her and say, "Adyn, stop! Don't parade that around and show all these people. That is pride in your heart. You need to keep that between you and me!" Not a chance.

Even writing that makes me feel wrong. As a dad, I would be so happy to see my daughter proudly sharing her work. I'd be pleased that she felt proud enough of what she worked on that she wanted to share it and tell her friends about her special connection with her daddy. I would probably sit there grinning like an idiot as she walked from kid to kid, sharing the work she is so proud of.

Why do we think God would feel any differently about us?

I believe God wants us to have pride. *What!* I know. It doesn't sound right. But I believe there is *good* pride and *bad* pride.

Let's start with bad pride. I think a better word is *hubris*. Hubris is dangerous overconfidence—the kind of pride that comes before a fall. If hubris could speak, it would tell you that you have it all figured out, that you are the expert everyone else should consult, that you don't need input or advice from friends, family, leaders, or even God. Hubris is incapable of celebrating other people's wins because it's threatened by their success. It views praise given to others as a diminishment of its own achievements. Hubris is self-centered. It keeps a record of wrongs others have committed to justify its own superiority. Hubris has a perpetually unsatisfied appetite for attention and accolades. Hubris is out of touch with reality.

Do I even need to say that this is bad pride? Probably not. We hear all the time about the bad pride. So what does *good* pride look like?

Good pride looks more like Adyn sharing her picture with

her classmates. When you're rocking good pride, you feel proud of your God-given talents. You want to share them because you understand where and in whom they originate. Good pride comes out when you create something that encourages other people—or more importantly, encourages you. It is forged out of relationship, love, and connection with Jesus. Good pride looks a lot like healthy humility. It's a humble confidence—confidence that enables you to praise other people for their work without feeling threatened. Confidence that gives you an uncritical spirit toward other people.

Stop apologizing for who you are. Stop hiding the beautiful gift inside you. The more you embrace your God-given authority, the less you will be threatened by someone else's. This is good pride.

✧ ✧

My friend Chris is an excellent musician. He's played all over the world and is one of the sharpest and most intuitive musicians I've ever had the pleasure to play with. He has done many things he's proud of and has spent a lot of years working to hone his craft. Because of him, I've met several other amazing and talented musicians—musicians whose technical ability and creativity in their craft blow me away.

But the thing about Chris that impresses me most is his positive, uncritical spirit. Anytime I mention another musician—literally anybody—he always has something positive to say. From rock to rap or bluegrass to country, he can find something to appreciate about anyone. He appreciates lyrics or melody lines. He enjoys bass grooves or technical skill. I always get the impression from Chris that he is so secure and proud of his own craft that he doesn't have the need or desire to criticize someone else's.

He once told me that the best musicians are often the least critical of other musicians because they have done the hard work themselves. If you're a guitarist who has spent hours practicing scales, you'll appreciate Joe Satriani's mad skills. If you have slogged out years of songwriting, you'll probably appreciate Bob Dylan or the Beatles. If you work at building strong hooks and catchy songs, you'll probably appreciate Taylor Swift or Justin Bieber.

Pride in your work—especially hard work—softens you toward others and makes it easier to celebrate their work. If you've worked hard to build a business from scratch, you will appreciate the success of someone else who has done the same. If you've worked hard to get your PhD, you will appreciate the achievements of someone who has overcome the difficulties of academic success. If you couple that appreciation with an understanding that God has created impressive skills, talents, and giftings in your own life, good pride happens. And it will enable you to genuinely celebrate those around you.

It's always a good idea to ask God to sift your heart and your motives. But if you have worked hard to create something—a church, a book, a business, a podcast, a mathematical theorem— sharing it with the world around you is not wrong. Let me say it again: if you have something you are proud of, it is not sin to promote it. Get it out there! Show people. Don't wrap your identity around how many people like it; wrap your identity around the God who gave you the gifts to begin with. But don't feel ashamed about your gifts and hard work, and don't feel bad about telling others about it.

This is what fostering influence is all about: building relation-ships on the genuine and heartfelt foundation of celebrating the influence we each have. Every one of us comes to the table with a group of people we influence. At some point, if you want your dream to take off, you need to build genuine relationships with people who can help you. But it's not built on the unhealthy pride; it's built on a humility to admit that you need other people. And it's built on a healthy pride rooted in God-soaked identity.

Grow in your ability to humbly network, and you will see your dream take major steps forward. But don't neglect the last step in getting your plan started. This next step is counterintuitive, but it's built on the backward nature of Jesus's kingdom.

CHAPTER 10

SERVE

When Blake and I first got married, she put a Bible verse up on some shelves above our toilet. Now, if you want a man to memorize something, print it out and put it above the toilet. He will see it *a lot*. Here's the verse: "Whatever you do, work at it with all your heart, as working for the Lord, not for human masters, since you know that you will receive an inheritance from the Lord as a reward. It is the Lord Christ you are serving" (Colossians 3:23–24).

Maybe I drank too much coffee or have a small bladder, because I ended up looking at this verse regularly. And the principle of working with all my heart as working for the Lord became a compass I learned to follow in that critical season of my life.

ALL HEART IN ALL THINGS

At the time, I was on staff at a small church of about 150 people. I led worship every Sunday and had a small team. And I loved it. I wasn't motivated by pay—it wasn't much—or the potential of moving up the ladder. I just loved it.

One of the things I had a reputation for in those days was leading long midweek worship practices. Part of the reason they were long was because I didn't manage my time well. Part of it was that our sound guy had to use string and tinfoil to get our RadioShack sound system working. But most of the problem was that I wanted us to *nail* every song. I was a perfectionist with a team that, well, wasn't perfect.

We had singers who spent their days selling real estate, not getting vocal lessons, and guitar players who were just learning on their Ibanez 7-string complete with Line 6 multi-effects pedal—sorry, inside musician jargon. We had a drummer who played AC/DC covers in bars on the weekend, so all our emotive, worshipful ballads started to feel more like "Highway to Hell." It was a lot of work to pull that team together.

I remember hitting a wall many rehearsal nights, and inevitably someone would pipe up, "Ryan, I think it's good enough." They were right. After two hours of rehearsal, I had gotten the best I could get out of my team that night, and I had to let them go home.

The struggle of the perfectionist.

But even as a young leader, I knew that the effort I put into that small church mattered and that how I treated that small team then would be how I treated a big team later. I was doing everything I could to walk in the Colossians 3:23–24 way of life—to do all things as working for the Lord. Not some things or just the "big" things, but all things. And it paid off in so many ways. The work ethic and motivation I developed for that small worship team in Tucson, Arizona, became the same work ethic and motivation I used for the bigger things later in life. From writing to touring, the effort I put in now is the same as the effort I put in when I was leading at that small church.

This all-your-heart-in-all-things principle is crucial for the dreamer to grasp.

Following your dreams is not something that's compartmentalized and hermetically sealed off for your future. It's here and now. How you work and lead now is how you will work and lead later. The degree of integrity you have in the small things now is a foreshadowing of the integrity you will have in the greater things later.

So far, so good, right? In fact, this is a principle that makes for a great quote on social media. It creates a nice applause line at a conference. But let's shift gears a bit and consider a question that may not make you want to post a quote and clap.

How well are you serving your current boss or leader?

Maybe you have a boss who doesn't encourage you or invest in you. Maybe you're serving under a leader who seems inept or unhealthy. Maybe your boss has lots of issues—things that frustrate you or keep you up at night because you're convinced you know a better way.

If your boss has imperfections that frustrate you, you might find yourself slacking off in your commitment—to them or to your job. I mean, this leader is small potatoes, right? And in the grand scheme of things, who cares about the work you do at a small business, a coffee shop, or a church? Why waste your time submitting to your boss's flawed leadership or working hard? That won't advance you up the ladder, so why does it matter how you serve?

This is where your faith needs to enter the scene. In God's economy, how you treat your imperfect leader right now *does* matter. It's one of the most important challenges you have. If we believe, truly believe, that we are working for the Lord—that he is the one who sees us and brings advancement and promotion—then how we treat any boss matters. How you treat your current boss is how you will treat your next boss, and your next boss after that.

What you also need to consider is this: if you foster a contentious culture of us-versus-them with your boss, even if it's in private, this culture will most likely trickle down. Meaning this: often times the way you treat your boss comes full circle, and it becomes how your followers follow you. In God's economy, the judgement we throw at our boss becomes the very same judgement thrown back at us. This is a principle Jesus taught us. In Matthew 7:2 he warns us not to judge another person. He says, "In the same way you judge others, you will be judged, and with the measure you use, it will be measured to you." He's saying that your judgement comes back to you. It is a sort of, forgive me here, Jesus karma in your attitude and judgement toward others. So the judgement and harsh expectations you hurl at your boss tend to come right back at you. In the same way, if you learn to follow with grace, commitment, and hard work, you will most likely inherit followers who do the same.

In light of all of that, here are a few more hard questions to consider:

1. Does your current leader know that you are behind him or her?
2. How do you think your boss would describe you and your work when you aren't in the room?
3. Would your boss miss you if you left?

You need to take questions such as these seriously. When you have a job to do, it's not all about how nurtured and cared for you feel; it's also about how nurtured and cared for your boss feels.

God is always at work in your work, even when you can't see it. Even when your leader isn't the greatest. Even when you are serving a small-potatoes leader. You are working for God—and sometimes promotion from God can feel like no-motion or even de-motion. Your character is like a diamond—it is forged under pressure. And how you act in a no-motion or de-motion job will foreshadow how you act when a job promotion comes your way.

✧ ✧

Let's touch base with our biblical dreamer, Joseph.

Joseph dreamed that he would be an influential man—that even his parents and brothers would bow before him. But before his dream is realized, Joseph's life goes down the toilet. His brothers fake his death and sell him into slavery. He is falsely accused and thrown into prison. People who promise to help him don't. By all indications, his life is going nowhere.

This is a fun story to read because we know Joseph will triumph a couple of chapters later, but it wasn't a fun story when Joseph was living it year after year. He could have easily chosen to wallow in self-pity and given up. And he would have been completely justified in doing so. Any good friend or psychologist would have told Joseph he was right to be angry. His family had abused him. Had left him out and ridiculed him. Had sold him as if he were property and had ruined his life forever.

And yet somehow Joseph doesn't give up. He doesn't give in to victimhood or bitterness. He doesn't allow the injustices against him to steal what he still has—pride in his work and faith in his God. Here's what happens right after he is sold into slavery by his brothers.

As it turned out, GOD was with Joseph and things went very well with him. He ended up living in the home of his Egyptian master. His master recognized that GOD was with him, saw that GOD was working for good in everything he did. He became very fond of Joseph and made him his personal aide. He put him in charge of all his personal affairs, turning everything over to him. From that moment on, GOD blessed the home of the Egyptian—all because of Joseph. The blessing of GOD spread over everything he owned, at home and in the fields, and all Potiphar had to concern himself with was eating three meals a day. (Genesis 39:2–6 MSG)

The text says his master notices that God is working through Joseph and that everything he does prospers and carries the mark of God on it. This didn't happen through prayer and faith alone. This happened with hard, faithful, and engaged work amid a dark and unjust situation. It was the result of Joseph pouring himself into his imperfect situation with everything he had, not to climb the ladder—because there was no ladder for him to climb—but to be faithful to the God he believed in and trusted.

Here's another principle to note about this part of Joseph's story, and it's one we have to read between the lines a bit to see. Joseph worked hard to serve his master and was promoted. He moved up in Potiphar's organization till he was in charge. This doesn't happen to passive-aggressive or insubordinate followers. This happens to people who know how to be themselves but still serve their leader. His submission and hard work led to promotion. His serving someone else in authority ultimately led to his becoming to one of the most powerful leaders in Egypt.

Submission precedes authority in Joseph's life. But because the word *submission* has been abused so much, it's hard to discern the difference between healthy submission and unhealthy submission. We have to dive into what submission is and what it isn't.

WHAT SUBMISSION IS

In the early days of my leadership, I served under a leader who was young like I was. He was strong; I was strong. He had opinions; I had opinions. Needless to say, we had our clashes. As the worship pastor, I had certain things I wouldn't compromise on. And since I was an immature leader, I had *a lot* of those.

One of my little rules was that I would never play secular songs on stage. I suppose I imagined that my gift in music was so pure that I should never defile it by playing anything but worship songs. Wherever I picked it up, it wasn't a rule expressly found in the Bible, and my commitment to it was steeped in a self-righteousness that I couldn't see at the time.

So, as you might have already guessed, one day my leader called to ask whether I would play a secular **gasp** song on Sunday. I had been preparing for this moment and had all my theological ducks in a row. I replied that I wouldn't. I *couldn't*. I went into my ninety-five theses on the subject and seasoned the whole conversation with a smug dash of self-righteous indignation.

When we got off the phone, I was confident that I had made my point. Surely he would see the error of his ways and relent to my thoroughly biblical justification for denying his request. Surely he would submit his philosophy to my better-thought-out one. I mean, how *couldn't* he?

The next day, I found out that he had gone around me and asked another one of my worship leaders to play the song. Cue explosion, drama, and fallout. Whenever pride is involved—especially the self-righteous, Bible-wrapped variety—relational breakdowns are sure to follow. Pride inflates small issues into big issues. Pride distorts reality. Pride feels entitled. Pride cannot share the same space with love or humility. Pride *cannot* submit to leadership.

This relational crash ultimately led me to leave the church. It was the first and last time I ever left a church in such a way. And it was more isolating and painful than I could ever have imagined. I'm not proud of it, but I am glad for it. It taught me the value of being committed to a church. It showed me the ugliness of what I'm capable of when I'm more committed to my pride than I am to my leader. And as a leader, it has shown me the warning signs of pride I need to pay attention to in those who report to me.

Was my boss a young and imperfect leader? Yes. Did he have areas he needed to grow in? Absolutely. But was he unbiblical or unreasonable to expect me to submit to his leadership? No.

And though I too was young and inexperienced, I did understand this one clear principle: if I couldn't submit to his leadership—as imperfect as it was—I had to leave. I couldn't continue to undermine him or create division in the camp. If I couldn't support him, *I* was the one who had to go.

✧ ✧

I had a hard time with the idea of submission. I think every immature leader does. And notice I say *immature* and not young. You can be fifty or seventy and still be an immature leader.

I think North American leaders have an especially difficult time with the word *submit*. When I raise the idea, people immediately tend to get defensive and want to put all kinds of qualifications around it. They feel obligated to say that submission to bad or unhealthy leaders is not required. We North Americans are a freedom-loving bunch. We love our independence. We don't like anyone to tell us what to do, especially a boss or a board we deem unworthy of our submission.

Are there bad leaders you should separate yourself from? Yes. I will go through some of the criteria for that in a bit. But for now, let's go to the book of Hebrews. "Obey your leaders and submit to them, for they are keeping watch over your souls, as those who will have to give an account. Let them do this with joy and not with groaning, for that would be of no advantage to you" (Hebrews 13:17 ESV).

Read that last bit again: "Let them do this with joy and not with groaning, for that would be of no advantage to you." In other words, don't make it a chore for them to lead you. Being a constant pain in your leader's side will not teach them a lesson; it will serve only to make your life under their leadership harder. It will be of no advantage to you.

That's the choice Joseph made—he served well under good leaders and bad. When he served his slave master well, the master took notice of his strong work ethic and promoted him. When he served Pharaoh well, Pharaoh recognized Joseph's supernatural wisdom and leadership and gave him more and more responsibility. Joseph worked hard. He worked fully invested and engaged. And he let God bring the promotion.

Take your focus off the imperfections of your current leader for a minute. Do your leaders recognize Joseph's attributes in your life? Are you someone they can trust to get things done? Are you a leader who displays the fruit of Jesus in your work?

Here is the thing us dreamers need to remember: we will never have a strong team of others serving our dream until we go strong to serve someone else's dream. A heart-posture of service toward your leader now will lead to a heart-posture of service from those who report to you in the future. This is that Jesus karma coming back around again. This is your faith impacting your ability to serve someone else's dream. If you believe that God sees, and is the one who promotes in his time, then you will serve him well by serving your current leader well.

Develop a habit of consistently praying for your current leader. Ask Jesus how you can serve this person better. Write those things down, and then do them.

WHAT SUBMISSION ISN'T

Submitting to a leader with whom you have issues isn't easy. No leader is perfect. No organization is without its challenges. And there are times when you should *not* submit to a leader. If they are taking advantage of people, you should not submit to them. If they are abusing you in any way—physically, sexually, verbally, emotionally—you should not submit to them. If they are breaking the law in any way, you should not submit to them. You need not only to leave but also to *report them*. Such behavior isn't only bad leadership or questionable theology, it is *wrong*. Submitting to such a leader will lead to damage and destruction, and you cannot tolerate it. Submission is *not* putting up with abusive or criminal behavior.

Submission is also not something that can be dictated. In other words, if your leader has to remind you to submit, there's a problem. Good leaders create an atmosphere in which people *want* to submit to their leadership. They cast a compelling vision and try to bring out the best in those serving under them.

Submission is not powerlessness. Submission to a leader is not laying aside your power or opinion; it's putting your strengths in service to another person's vision. It's leveraging your time, effort, and gifts for someone else.

Author and pastor John Piper said that the word *submission* in the context of Hebrews 13:7 is more accurately understood this way:

> I should have a bent towards trusting [my] leaders. Be bent that way. Don't be a distrustful people. Second, I should have a disposition to be supportive in my attitudes and actions toward the goals and the direction of the leaders. If they craft a vision and they set some goals, be supportive. Go with them. I think it means we should want to imitate their faith and I think it means we should have a happy inclination to comply with their instructions.[1]

Every leader requires grace. But if you find yourself in a situation in which it is impossible to follow your leader, you have to confront that head-on. As I learned the hard way, when I find myself set against a leader because of different styles or philosophies, I have to honor Jesus by honoring the position in which he has placed that leader. That means I have to either submit myself to this leader or leave. Resisting their authority, trying to steal their position, or stirring up trouble to get leverage over them will only hurt me, the leader, and everyone else in the organization.

If you cannot serve your leader and be a joy to them, be honest with them and yourself and start planning your exit.

But remember, the grass may look greener on the other side, but it rarely is. Nowhere is perfect. *Nowhere.* So if you are leaving because of leadership philosophy differences or because you keep comparing the organization you're in with one you follow on social media, you should pause. Choosing to leave a leader or organization could be more difficult than you realize. Wherever you end up, you will be starting from scratch. You'll need to build new connections and relational trust. Chances are high that the things you don't like in the current job will follow you to the next one. So don't be too quick to give up and move on. We often don't fully appreciate what we have until it's gone. Many times we lack appreciation for the thing right in front of us because we yearn for a perfection we will never fully find.

SERVE STRONG, LEAD STRONG

At this point, maybe you're wondering, *Why are you talking about submission to leadership in a book about pursuing dreams?*

If so, I'm glad you asked.

People who serve strong, lead strong. This is the upside-down nature of the kingdom of God. As dreamers, this is where our faith is put to the test. Do we believe—truly believe—the Colossians 3 mindset—that we are called to do all things as if working for God himself? Do we serve that way in our current role? This is the place we need to start as head-in-the-clouds dreamers. We start with our feet on the ground. We start right where we're at.

If your current role isn't your dream role, you may have this nagging feeling you're wasting your time. That you have bigger fish to fry. That your current assignment is not as big or as important as it should be. You may feel that your current leader doesn't nurture or appreciate you or that staying faithful where you are is somehow giving up. But it's not. Faithfulness is the secret weapon of the dreamer who wants to succeed. Promotion comes through faithfully serving—not just mindlessly sucking it up and surviving but *thriving* in your season of serving. And the only way to thrive in your current season is to be fully committed and engaged. The apostle Paul says it this way:

> So here's what I want you to do, God helping you: Take your everyday, ordinary life—your sleeping, eating, going-to-work, and walking-around life—and place it before God as an offering. Embracing what God does for you is the best thing you can do for him. Don't become so well-adjusted to your culture that you fit into it without even thinking. Instead, fix your attention on God. You'll be changed from the inside out. Readily recognize what he wants from you, and quickly respond to it. Unlike the culture around you, always dragging you down to its level of immaturity, God brings the best out of you, develops well-formed maturity in you. (Romans 12:1–2 MSG)

God wants to bring out the best in you and develop well-formed maturity in you—*now*. The job you have right now is no accident. The organization in which you serve is no accident.

There is a purpose for your role there. You may feel like Joseph in Potiphar's house, but you won't be able to live into your dream potential until you treat Potiphar's house as you hope to one day treat Pharaoh's house. This is the sacrificial life of the dreamer. This is the part where you die to yourself in pursuit of your God-given dream. I know! It sounds backward, but pursue your dream now by staying right where you are. I don't mean stay where you are spiritually or in your current skill level, but stay where you are *and* treat it as if it's somewhere new. Give it new effort. Give your leaders new commitment.

Sometimes serving at home is the hardest challenge you will face. Believe me, I know this from experience.

A couple of years back, my pastor David Stockton came to an OUTCRY event. He hung out backstage and joined our backstage prayer times. I was so proud to have him and the rest of my church team there. It felt as though I finally got to show my family what I was doing on tour. After the night was over, David and I talked, and he encouraged me. But after all the niceties were out of the way, he asked me what may be one of the most important questions I've ever been asked. "Ryan, how come you don't lead at home like you do here?"

Ouch.

It was a question that stopped me in my tracks, and I had no idea how to respond. To clarify, he wasn't asking because he felt as though I was slacking off somehow at home. He was asking because he recognized gifts and abilities in me that he hadn't seen me use at home. And when he asked the question, I had to ask myself even more questions.

Why do I feel freer to lead in a roomful of strangers than I do at home? Why am I a stronger leader in a roomful of people who intimidate me? Why have I buried my gifts so much at home? Why am I waiting for permission to be me?

When I got home from that tour, I determined this one simple thing: I was going to lead at home as I did on tour. So I treated our preservice meetings as OUTCRY meetings. I treated staff meetings as though they mattered. Because—I freshly realized—they did.

And things began to shift. Our meetings got better. Our preservice times became more meaningful and passionate, not because I suddenly became an awesome leader but because I stopped apologizing for who I am as a leader. I stopped treating my daily and weekly tasks as if they were inconsequential. I treated every week as if I were on an OUTCRY tour. And I began to value my leadership gift and use it. I am determined to never again let fear dictate how I lead.

God gives us a spark, but we determine when and where to start the fire. He gives us gifts and talents, but it's our choice whether or not we use them. One of the most challenging places to use and develop our gifts is at home. But giving our best at home will yield the greatest and longest-lasting fruit.

STARTING YOUR DREAM

When I started writing this book, it was going to be a book about creativity rather than dreams. I wanted the church to value creativity and see it as a central part of living out our God-given calling to create as God created. It was—and still is—something I am passionate about. But as I began to write, I found myself veering off onto other topics and issues. The more I wrote, the more my book on creativity turned into something else.

One day, after six months of struggling every day to write about creativity, I was with my family on vacation in California when I had a breakthrough. That morning, I sat outside and read the story of Gideon. I had read it many times before, but suddenly I saw connections between Gideon and other biblical characters, such as Joseph and Noah and Nehemiah. And also connections to me. So that day, I wrote an outline for a new book—a book for dreamers, a book for people who have big dreams from God but need help on their journeys. The ideas came at me thick and fast, and I frantically typed as many notes as I could on my phone. When I was done, I titled my notes "Head in the Clouds, Feet on the Ground."

That day, I wrote the rough outline for this book.

At the time, I thought I would write it after I published the creativity book. But after a few more months of struggling to write that first book, I paused and asked a scary question. It was scary because I already knew the answer. But I mustered my courage and prayed, "God, do you want me to write the book on creativity or the book on dreams." God clearly and swiftly answered, "The one on dreams." I took a deep breath and said, "Okay, God." A yes to God often means a no to something else. Sometimes a yes from God means you have to set aside something you've been pouring your heart into so you can pursue the new thing God reveals to you.

That day, I set aside nine months of work and started with a blank document. One of the scariest things an author can look at is that blinking cursor on a blank screen. I had to not only conquer a lot of fear to start over but also had to tell my publisher that I wanted to dump our nine months of work and start over. It was painful and frightening, but I knew I had to do it.

A month later, I had written more than I had in the previous nine months combined. I saw it so clearly. The foundation for cultivating a life of creativity is the pursuit of wholeness in your relationship with Jesus. This leads to confidence in who you are and what you uniquely bring to the world, a confidence born out of real confidence in the One who made you. This confidence of identity leads to a confidence in calling. It also leads to healthy expectations. Then you are equipped to face and overcome the dream killers that will inevitably arise.

And now that we've covered all that, you are in the same place you were when you started this book. In the same *location*. But hopefully with a new disposition. As you pursue your dream, the best preparation is being present and committed to whatever it is God has for you *now*. But when you face it with confidence and stretch your faith, this is not wasted time. Keep your dreams ever in front of you, but know where you stand.

My prayer for you is this: That you would be ever-dreaming and ever-hoping for the future and, at the same time, ever-expecting greater things from God in the present. That you would know who *you* are and who *God* is. That you would know deep down that your God-given identity is the source of peace and confidence in your life. That the childlike dreamer in you will come alive and lead you into even greater dreams than you can imagine. That you would embrace your creative genius and follow wherever it may lead you. In the end, I pray that you will truly know the joy and adventure of keeping your head in the clouds and your feet on the ground.

ACKNOWLEDGMENTS

This book developed from many years and experiences but ultimately came from *three* major influences in my life.

First my parents—Bob and Sue. My dad, being an entrepreneur and small business owner, taught me how to keep dreaming and pursuing that dream with unbridled optimism. My mom was always the common sense in the room of my dreamer father. And both of them were a team. They were both needed. One had his head in the clouds, the other had her feet on the ground. I am infinitely thankful for the lessons they taught me in their life, and most of them come to play throughout this book.

The second influence is my church, along with my pastor David Stockton. Being a part of Living Streams Church has grounded me in Scripture and taught me the value of building a spiritual foundation before all else. It's the reason for the first third of this book.

Finally, the hours of conversation with my friend and fellow dreamer Shane Quick, the one who taught me the power of serving other people's dreams while keeping your own alive. And the leader who provided so many opportunities for me to grow that I gained a lifetime of experience in a few short years.

The philosophies and wisdom in this book rest on the foundation laid by all three of these in equal parts.

NOTES

Chapter 2: The Dreamer

1. Mark Batterson, *The Circle Maker: Praying Circles Around Your Biggest Dreams and Greatest Fears* (Grand Rapids: Zondervan, 2011), 45.
2. Study Focuses on Strategies for Achieving Goals, Resolutions, https://www.dominican.edu/dominicannews/study-highlights -strategies-for-achieving-goals.

Chapter 3: Creative Geniuses

1. Sandeep Venkataram, "How Unique Is Our DNA?" *Quora*, https://www.quora.com/How-unique-is-our-DNA, accessed April 2019.
2. Steve Jobs, quoted from a 1994 interview filmed by the Silicon Valley Historical Association and included in the *Steve Jobs* documentary. Sally McBurney and John R. McLaughlin, *Steve Jobs: Visionary Entrepreneur*, directed by Sally McBurney (2013).

Chapter 6: The Noise

1. Abraham Joshua Heschel, *The Sabbath: Its Meaning for Modern Man* (New York: Farrar, Straus and Giroux, 1951, 1979, 2005), 13.
2. Herbert A. Simon, "Designing Organizations for an Information-Rich World," *Computers, Communication and the Public Interest*,

University Press, 1971), 40–41.

3. Diana I. Tamir and Jason P. Mitchell, "Disclosing Information about the Self Is Intrinsically Rewarding," *Proceedings of the National Academy of Science of the United States of America* 109, no. 21 (May 22, 2012): 8038–8043, https://doi.org/10.1073/pnas.1202129109.

4. Kep Kee Loh and Dr. Ryota Kanai, "Higher Media Multi-Tasking Is Associated with Smaller Gray-Matter Density in the Anterior Cingulate Cortex," *PLS ONE* 9, no. 9 (September 24, 2014): e106698, https://doi.org/10.1371/journal.pone.0106698.

5. Tiffany Shlain, quoted in *Manage Your Day-to-Day: Build Your Routine, Find Your Focus, and Sharpen Your Creative Mind*, ed. Jocelyn K. Glei (Las Vegas: Amazon Publishing, 2013), 144–145.

Chapter 8: Work

1. Josephus Daniels, *The Wilson Era: Years of War and After: 1917–1923* (Chapel Hill, NC: University of North Carolina Press, 1946), 624.

2. Simon Sinek, *Start with Why: How Great Leaders Inspire Everyone to Take Action* (New York: Penguin, 2011), 39, 58.

Chapter 10: Serve

1. John Piper, "How Do I Obey and Submit to My Leaders?" *Ask Pastor John*, episode 201 (October 24, 2013), https://www.desiringgod.org/interviews/how-do-i-obey-and-submit-to-my-leaders.